DATE DUE

DATE DUE

Copyright 1999

PRINTED IN U.S.A.

Libya

Libya

BY TERRI WILLIS

Enchantment of the World
Second Series

Children's Press®

A Division of Grolier Publishing

NEW YORK   LONDON   HONG KONG   SYDNEY
DANBURY, CONNECTICUT

Frontispiece: Preparing tea in the Sahara

Consultants: Mohammed M. Aman, Ph.D., Dean and Professor, School of Library and
   Information Science, University of Wisconsin
   Amy J. Johnson, Ph.D., Assistant Professor of History, Berry College

Please note: All statistics are as up-to-date as possible at the time of publication.

Visit Children's Press on the Internet: http://publishing.grolier.com

Book design by Ox+Company, Inc.

Library of Congress Cataloging-in-Publication Data

Willis, Terri.
      Libya / by Terri Willis.
            p.   cm. — (Enchantment of the world. Second series)
      Includes bibliographical references (p.   ) and index.
      Summary: Describes the history, geography, economy, culture,
people, and religion of the North African country of Libya.
      ISBN 0-516-21008-4
      1. Libya—Juvenile literature. [1. Libya.] I. Title.
II. Series.
DT215.W55   1999
916.12—dc21   98-28174
                                                                                 CIP
                                                                                  AC

Libya

Contents

Cover photo:
A Tuareg man in the
Sahara Desert

The desert

A gazelle

CHAPTER
ONE

Riches Under the Sand

An oasis in the Fezzan Region

L IBYA IS AN ANCIENT LAND with a history reaching back over centuries. It is made up mostly of desert—90 percent of the nation's land is part of the Sahara, the world's largest desert. But despite its long history, the two greatest changes in Libya took place in the second half of the twentieth century. Both involve the rich resources below the surface of Libya's dry land.

One of these valuable resources is oil. Its oil transformed Libya from one of the world's poorest countries to one of the wealthiest. The other resource is groundwater. It is now being used to turn a barren landscape into a fertile area that may produce enough crops to feed the country—and even to export.

The people of Libya have learned to tap into the riches flowing beneath them. Today, they are transforming their nation.

Oil Is Found

Before 1959, Libya was very poor. It had been colonized—ruled by other countries—until 1951, and little had been done

Opposite: **D'Awbari sand dunes**

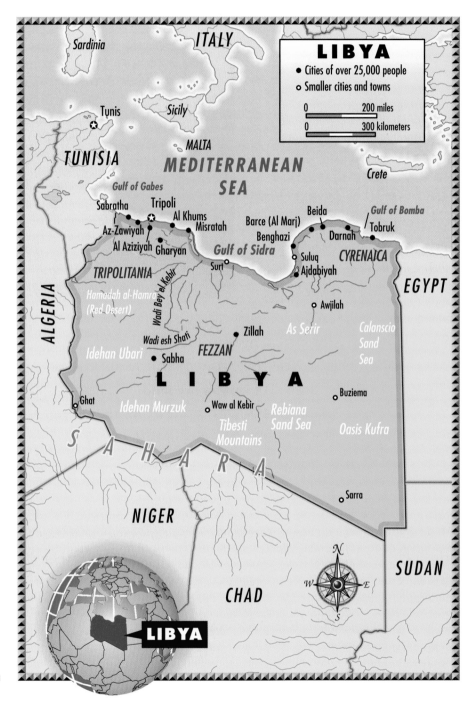

LIBYA
- Cities of over 25,000 people
- Smaller cities and towns

0   200 miles
0   300 kilometers

Sardinia

ITALY

Tunis

Sicily

TUNISIA

MALTA

MEDITERRANEAN
SEA

Crete

Gulf of Gabes

Sabratha   Tripoli
Az-Zawiyah   Al Khums
Al Aziziyah   Misratah
          Gharyan

Beida
Barce (Al Marj)
Benghazi
Darnah

Gulf of Bomba
Tobruk

Gulf of Sidra

Suluq
Ajdabiyah

CYRENAICA

EGYPT

Surt

TRIPOLITANIA

Hamadah al-Hamra
(Red Desert)

Awjilah

ALGERIA

Zillah

As Serir

Calanscio
Sand
Sea

Wadi esh Shati

FEZZAN

Idehan Ubari

Sabha

L I B Y A

Buziema

Ghat

Idehan Murzuk

Waw al Kebir

Rebiana
Sand Sea

Oasis Kufra

S A H A R A

Tibesti
Mountains

Sarra

NIGER

N
W   E
S

SUDAN

CHAD

LIBYA

Geopolitical map of Libya

10 *Libya*

to help the people of Libya. With few natural resources, it didn't seem like much could be done. Most people made their living by farming, selling a few small items in villages, or hunting and gathering what they could as they wandered across the desert. Some earned a living through trading across the vast Sahara. This was a risky business because many people died from the heat, and others were killed by thieves along their routes.

In June 1959, the cheers of joyful workers in the Libyan Desert signaled change. They had struck oil! Libya was on its way to becoming a major world economic force.

The oil strike didn't happen overnight. More than twenty years had passed from the time geologists first suspected that there might be oil under the desert until that eventful day in 1959. Thousands of men had toiled in the heat, risking their lives. At times, sudden desert storms covered their equipment in sand. In addition, millions of land mines added to the danger. The mines had been left buried in the desert following the battles for control of Libya during World War II (1939–1945).

After thousands of dollars were lost on potential oil wells that came up dry, it was Esso Oil Company that drilled the lucky well. There was reason to believe that a place in the Sahara named Jebel Zelten might be a likely spot. A few petrified palm tree trunks were found nearby, along with ancient shells that indicated a sea might have covered the area millions of years ago. These were promising signs, but Jebel Zelten looked a lot like every other dry well that had been dug.

A Libyan oil field

Yet when oil began to flow from that well, it really gushed! The Jebel Zelten well produced more than 15,000 barrels of oil per day. This was astonishing, when most wells in the United States produced only about 13 barrels a day. Even in oil-rich Iran, wells produced only about 5,300 barrels each. And the well at Jebel Zelten was only the first of many such wells drilled in Libya. Its great oil fields cover 600 miles (966 km) by 300 miles (483 km) across the Libyan desert.

El Hariega oil terminal

The oil strike came at a good time. In 1959, the number of cars was growing rapidly worldwide, and oil was needed to fuel those cars. The price of oil was rising, and Libya was ready to profit from it. Changes were felt throughout society.

Jobs were created. Salaries soared. New government programs were put into place to improve people's lives and to build the nation's military forces. Schools, health care, roads, communications, housing—oil supplied money to improve all of these. Today, oil continues to be the mainstay of Libya's economy.

Still, even with all the oil money flowing into the country, Libya has been unable to grow enough food to feed its citizens. Crops are grown along the northern coastline and in scattered oases in the desert, but most of the land is too dry to grow any fruits or vegetables. So Libya is turning to another great resource that flows beneath its sand—water.

The Great Man-Made River

Even though Libya borders the Mediterranean Sea, water for agriculture is in short supply. Seawater cannot be used to water crops because, as it evaporates, it leaves salt behind, and salt damages the soil. Most of the underground wells that supplied water to this land for centuries are now drying up or are becoming too salty as seawater seeps into them.

Since 1984, Libyans have been working on an enormous project that will tap into the large reserves of fresh water— called aquifers—under the desert. The water has been there, trapped between layers of rock and sand, for about 30,000 years. It slowly sifted down as the glaciers of the last ice age melted. Pipelines are now being built to carry the ancient water hundreds of miles north to Libya's farming region.

Called the Great Man-Made River, the project is still under construction. So far, more than 2,000 miles (3,219 km)

of pipe measuring 13 feet (4 m) across have been laid. Portions of the pipeline are already carrying water—from Tazerbo to Benghazi, from Sarir to Surt, and from southwestern Libya to the north. Today, more than 70 million cubic feet (2 million cubic m) of water are carried daily through the system.

More than 12,000 foreign workers are building the next portion, which will extend the pipeline to the Tripoli coastal region. This should nearly double the daily capacity of the system. Eventually, plans are for more than 3,000 miles (4,828 km) of pipeline, stretching across the nation.

The project is controversial. Some scientists predict that the underground wells will dry up in less than fifty years. Others say that pumping water to grow food in northern Libya will be too expensive and insist that it would cost less to buy the food from other countries. Still others say that draining the water from underground will weaken the land above the aquifers and cause serious damage from cave-ins. But Libya's leadership supports the program, pointing to the great benefits to agriculture, along with the many new jobs created to build the pipeline.

Only time will tell what the Great Man-Made River will do for Libya. No one yet knows whether its underground water will bring the hoped-for agricultural riches. But certainly, its underground oil has brought great wealth.

Opposite: **The inauguration of the Great Man-Made River project in Tripoli**

From Sea to Sand

LIBYA'S GREAT OIL FIELDS HELPED THE COUNTRY GAIN WORLD attention. When people think of Libya today, many conjure up images of huge oil rigs pumping away in vast stretches of swirling desert sand.

To some extent, they're right. The Sahara cuts across a wide area in southern Libya. But the desert is more than just sand—and Libya is more than just desert.

Libya's northern border is a beautiful coastline. Its green fields and sun-drenched beaches stretch more than 1,000 miles (1,600 km) along the Mediterranean Sea. High mountains reach toward the sky in the southwest. About 600 miles (970

Children helping out at the Susa port in Cyrenaica

km) of Libya's western border are shared with Algeria; another 250 miles (400 km), with Tunisia. The countries of Chad and Niger lie to the south of Libya. To the east, Libya shares a border of about 800 miles (1,287 km) with the Arab Republic of Egypt. Sudan, south of Egypt, is Libya's other eastern neighbor.

Libya's Geographical Features

Highest Elevation: Bikku Bitti (Bette Peak), 7,500 feet (2,286 m) above sea level

Lowest Elevation: Sabkhat Ghuzayyil, 154 feet (47 m) below sea level

Man-Made River: The Great Man-Made River, water pipeline more than 2,000 miles (3,219 km) long

Coastline: 1,100 miles (1,770 km)

Highest Annual Precipitation: 16 inches (40 cm), near Tripoli

Lowest Annual Precipitation: Less than 1 inch (2.5 cm), in the Sahara

Highest Recorded Temperature: 136°F (58°C), in Al-Aziziyah in 1922; the highest recorded world temperature in the shade

Highest Average Temperature: 88°F (31°C), at Sabha, in July

Lowest Average Temperature: 47°F (8°C), in Tripoli, in January

Greatest Distance North to South: 930 miles (1,497 km)

Greatest Distance East to West: 1,050 miles (1,690 km)

With 679,358 square miles (1,759,401 sq km) of land, Libya is Africa's fourth-largest country. Only Algeria, the Democratic Republic of the Congo, and the Sudan are larger. It covers more land than the states of Alaska and Minnesota combined.

Each of the nation's three regions—Tripolitania, Fezzan, and Cyrenaica—is marked by its unique geography. The natural boundaries that created these three distinct regions kept the cultures of each region separate for centuries. Until 1951, each region was an official province. Today, the three regions form Libya, a country of great diversity.

Tripolitania

Tripolitania makes up Libya's north-west region, from the Tunisian border eastward toward the Gulf of Sidra, and inland for several hundred miles. It covers about 110,000 square miles (285,000 sq km)—16 percent of Libya's total land. Part of Tripolitania is a swath of low-lying land, about 6 miles (9.7 km) wide and 186 miles (300 km) long, along the coast of the Mediterranean. Sand flats are common here, and there are also some marshy lagoons. This region also has vast stretches of coarse grass broken up by *wadis*—riverbeds that remain dry except during the rainy season, when they fill with water rushing toward the sea.

This coastline is an important agricultural region for the nation. Wheat, barley, cauliflower, and tomatoes are grown here, and groves of trees produce such crops as dates, almonds, olives, and citrus fruits. The city of Tripoli, Libya's capital, stands on this coast also. Nearly one-third of Libya's people live in and around Tripoli.

The Marble Arch

The white marble triumphal arch in Tripoli, Libya's largest city and capital, was built by the Romans about A.D. 163 to honor Marcus Aurelius. At that time, Rome controlled the region, and Marcus had become emperor of Rome a few years earlier. During that period, the Roman Empire seemed to be in decline. Its land was threatened by invading tribes, and poverty was growing among all but the top members of the upper class. Marcus restored much of the empire's glory. He was a good and honest ruler who put the well-being of his people ahead of his own welfare. He also passed laws to improve the lives of slaves and, although he was a peaceful man, he made sure that the Roman Empire had a strong military force to protect it from invaders. Marcus Aurelius died in 180.

Tripoli Harbor

Inland from the coast, the land slowly rises to merge with the Jefara Plains. The long, flat plains are scrubby and desert-like, until they reach the Jebel Nefusah, a series of limestone hills. Old craters and lava rocks found in the area indicate that these hills were created by volcanoes in ancient times. Today, the hills of the Jebel Nefusah, reaching to heights of about 3,000 feet (914 m), support little more than a few fig trees.

Traveling southward, the hills slowly taper off into the *Hamadah al-Hamra*, also known as the Red Desert. It gets its name from the red sandstone that forms its rocky plateau. It creates a flat landscape that sweeps across hundreds of miles until it eventually reaches the desert of Fezzan.

Fezzan is desert, and its 212,805 square miles (551,170 sq km) make up most of southwestern Libya. Here, vast sand dunes—some several hundred feet high—change shape slowly with the shifting wind. Called *ergs* in Arabic, these dunes cover about one-fifth of the land. Much of the rest is jagged, rocky plateau. The odd shapes that seem to grow up from some of the rocks are carved by the wind and the intense temperature changes of the desert.

The land is lower here, forming depressions called *sabkhas*, which look like large bowls on the desert floor. Many of these depressions contain underground water, which creates oasis areas.

Rocks in the desert form odd shapes because of the wind and temperature changes.

A Bedouin woman and child

Oases are the traditional lands of *nomads*—people who wander in search of grazing land for their animals and fresh supplies of food and water for themselves. These desert nomads, called *Bedouin*, find most of these resources on the oases. Very little grows in the desert except for a bit of scrubby vegetation. Few Libyans are nomads today—since the discovery of oil, most Bedouin have moved to the urban areas of northern Libya. But throughout most of the country's history, thousands of nomads found refuge on the oases, a pleasant change from the desert.

The desert is all that remains of a gigantic mountain range dating back more than 600 million years. These mountains were made up of granite, gneiss, schist, and quartzite. Over

Oases

An oasis is like a patch of green in the sea of sand. Its deep underground wells or springs provide enough water for trees, grass, and shrubs. In some large oases, villages have formed, and people grow crops. Smaller oases may be home to just a family or two.

time, the sea advanced over the region, and then retreated. Scientists have found evidence of this in marine fossils in the desert. Through the centuries, the water, the wind, and temperature changes worked together to erode the mountains, forming the sands and plateaus of today.

Most of Fezzan is fairly flat, but the Tibesti Mountains rise in the south along the border with Chad. These mountains include Bette Peak, the highest point in Libya at 7,500 feet (2,286 m).

Benghazi

Cyrenaica

Cyrenaica, the northeastern part of Libya, is the country's largest geographic region. At approximately 330,258 square miles (855,368 sq km), it covers nearly half of Libya. Here the eastern part of Libya's Mediterranean coast forms another rich agricultural area, providing fertile soil for vineyards and fruit trees. Here, too, are the cities of Benghazi, Darnah, and Tobruk. A large percentage of the Libyan people live in these important ports.

Looking at Libyan Cities

Benghazi lies at sea level in northeastern Libya on the Mediterranean Sea. Founded by Greeks about 515 B.C., Benghazi is Libya's second-largest city. The city is a center of oil refining as well as a busy seaport. Residents and visitors buy food and clothing at Souq al-Jreed, an outdoor market. Tourists also enjoy several nearby beaches. Benghazi's average temperature is 56°F (13°C) in January, and 77°F (25°C) in July. Its annual rainfall is 11 inches (28 cm).

Misratah, Libya's third-largest city, is located east of Tripoli in northwestern Libya. Misratah is separated from the Mediterranean Sea by some of the world's tallest sand dunes. The city began as a supply center for caravans about A.D. 800 and has been a trading center ever since. Today, groves of palm and olive trees surround the town. Misratah's main industry is based on two iron and steel mills, whose workers are mainly non-Libyans. Many craftspeople in Misratah make carpets, baskets, and pottery.

Az-Zawiyah, Libya's fourth-largest city, is located west of Tripoli. Oil and agriculture are the city's main businesses. Az-Zawiyah is near an important oil field and is the site of Libya's first oil refinery. Groundwater is also plentiful near Az-Zawiyah, so farmers there grow potatoes, onions, and tomatoes.

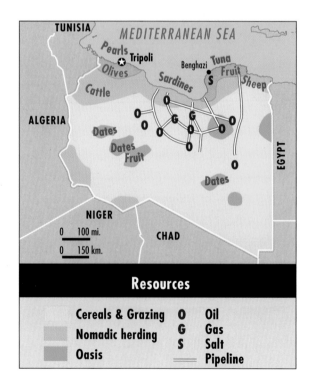

South of the coastline, the land rises steeply about 2,900 feet (880 m) to a rocky plateau called *Al-Jabal al-Akhda* (the Green Mountain). This name probably comes from the lovely flowers that cover the mountain's lower slopes—anemones, cyclamen, lilies, and narcissus. At higher elevations, scrubby shrubs and juniper grow. This plateau extends south all the way to the Libyan Desert, a part of the Sahara.

The reddish-brown Sand Sea of Calanscia in eastern Libya forms part of the Libyan Desert. One of the largest and most important oases in Libya is here—

Water

Libya has no rivers that flow all year round. Its rivers form during the rainy season following heavy downpours and flow to the sea in the wadis. The seawater must be desalinated—a process that removes salt—before it can be used for drinking and agriculture. Because desalination is expensive, it is not often done. But the vast aquifers that supply the water for the Great Man-Made River are already supplying about 60 percent of the country's water needs through the oases and the traditional pumping systems.

the Al-Kufrah. It was an important stop for the trans-Sahara trading caravans, and a place where nomads found the food and other resources they needed.

Libya's Climate

You might think that a country with such a variety of landscapes would have a variety of weather patterns too. But because most of Libya is desert, hot and dry weather comprises much of the climate.

Evaporation

In the desert, any water that falls as rain or rises up to the surface from aquifers evaporates rapidly because of the extremely dry air and heat. And water evaporates as rapidly from the human body as it does from the land. People can lose all their body fluids very quickly. People in the desert must drink from 14 to 26 pints (7 to 12 l) of water a day to avoid sickness. That's about 28 to 52 glasses of water each day! In the Sahara, a person can survive without water for only one day.

It's little surprise how hot it gets in the Sahara, with daytime temperatures in the summer averaging almost 100°F (38°C) and often reaching 115°F (46°C). But it's cooler in winter, with temperatures of only about 60 or 70°F (16 or 21°C). And in the high mountain ranges along Libya's southern border, it can get downright cold, with ice and snow on the ground at times.

Rainfall in the desert is light, about 4 inches (10 cm) per year, and as little as 2/10 inch (0.5 cm) some years. In the spring and fall, desert winds build up, carrying swirls of dust and sand all the way north to the Mediterranean Sea. These hot winds, called *ghiblis*, usually last one to four days. They damage the coastal cereal crops in the spring, but in the fall, their warmth speeds the ripening of the date crops.

The weather in Libya's coastal areas is affected by the Mediterranean Sea, and temperature and humidity vary between summer (June through September) and winter (October through May). Summers are hot and humid. Winters are much cooler, and most rain falls then—about 14 to 22 inches (36 to 56 cm) per year. Farther south, the plains region of Cyrenaica gets the heaviest rainfall—about 26 inches (66 cm) yearly. These rains often cause flash floods because the parched ground does not absorb moisture easily. The waters rush down ancient wadis toward the sea.

Opposite: **This family's cave dwelling is protected from cold winds in the winter and intense heat in the summer.**

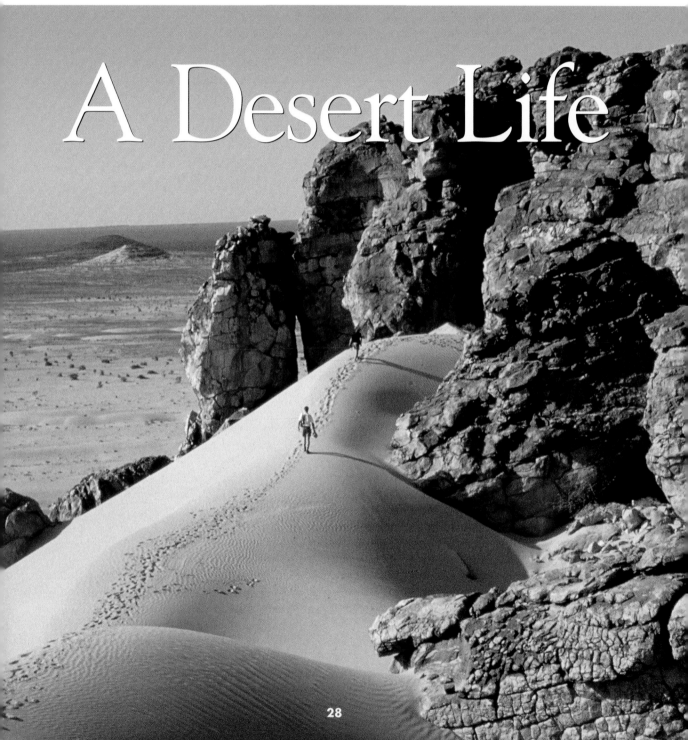

A Desert Life

THE MILD CLIMATE AND FERTILE LANDS OF LIBYA'S COASTAL region support a variety of plants and animals. But the desert climate of most of the nation presents challenges to living things. When we think of a desert animal, we usually think of the camel. It is often called "the ship of the desert."

For centuries, just as ships were the only means of transport across oceans, camels were the only means of travel across deserts. The camel is uniquely suited for the task, able to live for many days without water. But camels are not the only animals in Libya. There are jerboa and hyenas, gazelles, foxes, and wildcats. Poisonous snakes live in the oases. Larks and vultures are among the several types of birds.

The number of animals and the diversity of species found in Libya is much smaller than is found in rain forests or jungles, for example. Libya's animal population is not at all like that of a rain forest or a jungle. But considering the harsh climate in Libya, its animals are fairly plentiful. Let's begin with a look at the ship of the desert—the single-humped dromedary known as the camel.

A gazelle

The Camel

Camels were first introduced to North Africa in the first century A.D., when Persian invaders brought them to Egypt. In less than 100 years, they became common throughout the region.

The camel's ability to take in lots of water is well known: A camel can drink 25 gallons (95 l) at one time! It can store about 50 gallons (189 l) of water in three different sections of its stomach and live up to ten days without water. Its hump is a large lump of fat that is tapped when no other source of food or water is available. Camels have other features that allow them to thrive in the desert as well. They can close their eyes and nostrils so tightly during a windstorm that not a speck of sand blows in. They can live on the pits of date palms and thorny desert shrubs. The leathery soles of their feet are big and wide, just right for walking across both sandy and stony ground. And camels can smell water up to 1 mile (1.6 km) away!

Camels are prized by nomads for their ability to withstand desert conditions. They can carry up to 1,000 pounds (454 kg) at a time and are useful for plowing. Camel's milk can be used for drinking and to make cheese, and dried camel droppings make good fuel. The soft hair from their bellies can be woven into warm, strong cloth and used to make tents.

Ode to a Camel

Because camels were so important to the lives of nomadic people of the Libyan Desert in the past, they were revered. When visitors came, their camels' needs were met first, before their own. Nomads believed that people would be judged after death based on the kindness they showed to camels during life. And camels were often praised in nomadic folk songs and poetry:

> My camel is like lightning, the finest of animals;
> When it turns its head towards me
> Its hair feels soft as silk.

Opposite: **Camels are an important part of desert life.**

Since trucks have become more common in the desert today, nomads depend less on the camel. A person's wealth is no longer measured by the number of camels he owns. But the importance of the camel to the history of the nomadic people can never be overemphasized.

Other Desert Animals

Several other animals are specially suited to life in the desert, too. Some animals—especially rodents—adapt to the harsh climate through *estivation*—being inactive during the hot summer months. This is somewhat like *hibernation*, sleeping through the cold winter. Nighthawks and some insects also survive through estivation. Other animals, like the jerboa, are nocturnal, meaning they sleep during the day and hunt for food at night.

The jerboa is a small, mouselike creature that stays under the sand during the heat of the day and comes out to feed during the cooler nighttime. It hops like a tiny kangaroo, balancing with its 6-inch (15-cm) tail, nearly as long as its body.

A jerboa

Dressing for the Desert

Most mammals found in the Libyan Desert have light, sandy-colored fur and skin. They have developed this trait for two reasons. First, their light coloring blends in with the background of sand and rocks, so that their enemies have difficulty finding them. This natural process of blending in with the background is called camouflage. Second, light colors reflect light and heat. So their light coloring helps the desert animals stay cooler.

Some desert animals in Libya are also found elsewhere in the world, such as foxes, hyenas, and wildcats. These carnivores, or meat-eaters, constantly roam the desert hunting for prey. Fennec foxes, for example, get the water they need to survive by eating other desert animals and insects—especially jerboas. These desert foxes with huge ears also enjoy sweet fruits found in oases.

In the past, Libya had many desert gazelles, but they are rarely seen today because they were hunted so heavily. The addax antelope is still found near the Algerian border, living on the coarse

A fennec fox

The addax antelope is an endangered species.

grass and tough bushes. Weighing in at more than 400 pounds (181 kg), it travels easily over the sand on its wide hooves.

Many desert reptiles and arthropods are most active during the night. When the sun goes down, huge spiders, centipedes, and poisonous scorpions roam the desert floor along with grasshoppers and beetles. Some spiders keep the heat out of their homes by plugging their holes with sand when they get home.

Several types of lizards and poisonous snakes live in the Libyan Desert. These are cold-blooded reptiles. That means their temperature changes with their surroundings. At night, their bodies become so chilled that they need to get out in the sun each morning to warm up, before they sneak back below the sand. Chameleons and other lizards—some more than 3 feet (1 m) long—are among the desert dwellers. Varans, the region's largest and most powerful lizards, use their spiked tail as weapons. A common lizard

The desert is home to spiders that are usually active at night.

An emperor scorpion

found in Libya is the skink. It uses its wedge-shaped jaw to dig holes in the sand to hide in and cool off. Its eyes are covered with transparent scales that prevent irritation from the sand.

Snakes include the horned viper, Cleopatra's asp, and adders. Brightly colored kraits can easily be seen against the dull sand and rocks during the light of day, but they move around at night when they can easily sink their grooved fangs into unsuspecting victims.

Birds of the desert include vultures and hawks. The sandgrouse is also well suited for life in a dry climate. Its water-absorbing feathers allow the adult birds to carry moisture back to their nests to cool their eggs.

Adapting to the Desert

Many animals, birds, and reptiles of the desert have adapted to a life of little water with an unusual urination process. These mammals expel very concentrated urine, with little water mixed in, keeping most water in their bodies. Some desert birds and reptiles do not excrete liquid urine at all, just concentrated crystals of uric acid.

Animals living in the oases have an easier life than the desert-dwellers do. Oases shelter many house mice and rats, as well as bats and several types of birds, such as warblers, larks, grouse, desert bullfinches, and turtledoves. Butterflies and dragonflies fly overhead and sometimes venture out into the desert for a time.

The wadden, a male gazelle, is Libya's national animal. Wadden are fairly plentiful along Libya's northern coastal region and are often seen wandering about the countryside.

Plant Life

Just as animals in desert regions must adapt to the environment, so too must plants. They need to be able to survive the hot, dry conditions, and to grow in land that is often very salty. Typically, desert plants have long root systems that tap into groundwater far below the surface, and most have small leaves or spiny thorns, from which little moisture evaporates. Several plants, too, are *halophytes*—plants that thrive in salty soils.

Most plants found in Libya's portion of the Sahara are similar to desert plants everywhere. But the Sahara has fewer kinds of plants than most other deserts. A few scrubby grasses are found here and there, but there are very few trees outside of the oases.

Throughout Libya and its oases, many cactus plants and palm trees grow wild. Date palm trees thrive even under the extreme heat of summer and chilling frost of winter. These trees are useful in many ways—dates are a delicious fruit, fresh or dried. They can be ground into flour, and their sweet juice

There are fewer types of plants in the Sahara than in most deserts.

makes a treat similar to honey. The palm tree trunks are used for lumber and fuel. And the palm fronds themselves are woven into sandals, baskets, and mats. No part of the date palm is wasted.

Date palm trees grow wild throughout Libya.

The cactus is Libya's national plant. The prickly pear cactus has a sweet, juicy fruit that many people enjoy. Wild pistachios are another treat. And grass grows in most non-desert areas. Esparto grass, in particular, is used to make paper and rope. Libya once exported much Esparto grass. The Asphodel lily, used in cooking, is one of the many herbs that grow in Libya's coastal region. Henna shrubs are used to make red dye, often used for hair. Many Libyan women use henna to dye their hair and some use it to paint intricate designs on their hands.

Dye from henna shrubs is used to adorn women's hands with intricate designs.

In a land where the number and types of animal and plant life are limited by the environment, people must learn to make use of them in every way possible. The people of Libya have learned to do this very well.

The Lush Desert

In the rare times when heavy rains fall in the Sahara—usually less than once in ten years—the desert blossoms. Grasses, herbs, and flowers spring up. The seeds and bulbs that produce them can survive long, hot, dry periods and still produce plants, but the water they need is not usually available.

Young Nation, Ancient Land

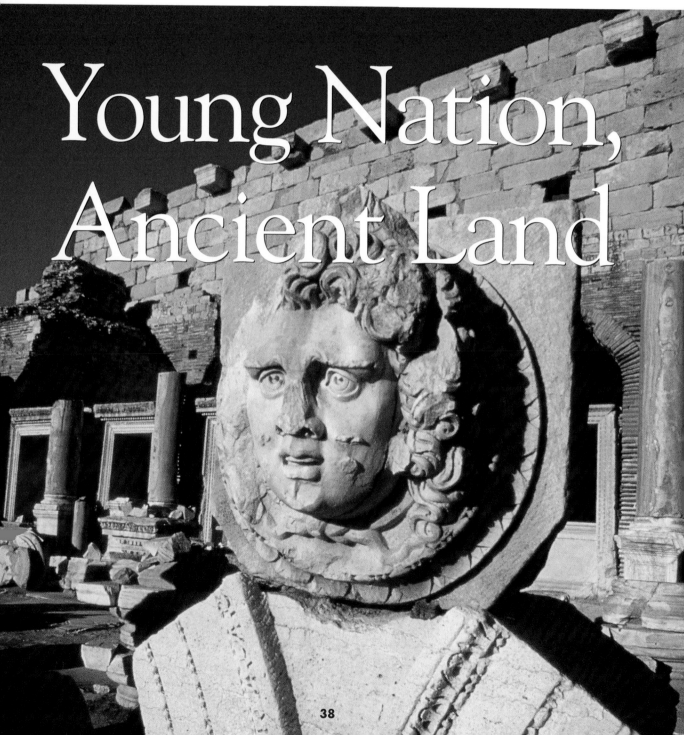

L IBYA, AS A NATION, IS QUITE YOUNG. IT BECAME AN independent nation, the Kingdom of Libya, in 1951. Before that date, it was a colony made up of three provinces ruled by many different nations over time. Even more recently, in 1969, it became known as the Libyan Arab Republic, and in 1977 it got its present name: the Socialist People's Libyan Arab Jamahiriya. *Jamahiriya* is an Arabic term meaning a "state representing the interests of the great masses."

Still, Libya is an ancient land. Its people have a history rich with stories of kingdoms and wars and difficulties overcome.

A prehistoric rock engraving of a crocodile

Early Inhabitants

More than 10,000 years ago, prehistoric rock artists drew pictures in each of Libya's three regions. They depicted an environment very different from today's Libya. The artists drew landscapes full of plants—grasses, shrubs, evergreens, and many kinds of trees. They included large herds of animals living near flowing rivers and lakes. Crocodiles, hippopotamuses, zebras, ostriches, and even elephants and

There were fewer takeovers in Fezzan than in Tripolitania and Cyrenaica because its land was less attractive to conquering nations. In Fezzan, the Garamantes ruled from about 1000 B.C. A strong, warlike tribe, they controlled much of the trade route across the Sahara, as caravans brought ivory and gold from deep in Africa north to the Mediterranean. Pyramid tombs built by the Garamantes still stand today.

giraffes are seen in the pictures. These animals have not lived in northern Africa for thousands of years.

The ancient artists were drawing the world around them—there are fossil remains of such plants and animals left behind to prove it. Scientists believe that the deserts of Libya were once jungle. Early humans could find all the food they needed by hunting and gathering. They were nomads who traveled throughout the region in search of food.

Later, around 5000 B.C., the people learned to cultivate plants and raise cattle. As farmers, they were able to live in one place. These original settlers of Libya were known as Berbers. The term *berber* comes from the Latin word for "barbarian." The name was given to the people of northeastern Africa who did not speak Latin by the Romans who took over the region in 46 B.C. Berber tribes still live throughout North Africa today.

The Berbers' fertile lands were valuable. They became a target for warring nations to conquer and control, especially along the Mediterranean coast in the regions of Tripolitania and Cyrenaica.

Outsiders in Charge

Phoenician sailors, from the area that is now Lebanon, established ports on Libya's Mediterranean coast in Tripolitania beginning in 1300 B.C. They wanted sites to anchor ships along their trade route from Phoenicia to Spain. Though they reigned for the next 500 years, they did little to colonize the region. They had no need to travel farther inland for resources

or to establish communities. Instead, the small Phoenician settlements along Libya's coast remained dependent upon their homeland for leadership and supplies.

The Phoenicians did found the city of Carthage, however, farther west along North Africa's coast, on land that is now part of Tunisia. Its ideal location as a Mediterranean seaport made Carthage one of the wealthiest cities of its time, and an independent power in its own right. Carthage built up a strong military force, and soon Carthaginians ruled much of the Mediterranean's North African coast, including Tripolitania.

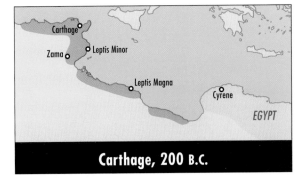

Carthage, 200 B.C.

Unlike the Phoenicians, the Carthaginians established several colonies. They were harsh rulers. Some of the strongest men were forced to fight for the Carthaginians, while the rest of the citizens were put to work farming and forced to give their rulers as much as half of their crops each season.

Few permanent settlements built by the Carthaginians remain today. The most prosperous cities of the time were stopping points in the trade route across the Sahara, linking the Mediterranean Sea with the Niger River. Along that route, dealers exchanged valuable gemstones, fine cloth, foods, slaves, and other goods. Over time, the trade route faded due to wars and lack of resources, and the cities faded with it.

Leaving a Mark on the Land

The next groups to rule Libya built great cities and monuments, some of which remain. Archaeologists have found ruins to prove that both the Greeks and the Romans had a strong presence in the region.

Ruins of Roman Carthage

Romans established themselves in 46 B.C., when they took over the Carthaginian Empire. Tripolitania's coastal region became one of the main sources of grain and other foods for the Roman Empire.

The Greek stronghold in ancient Libya was in Cyrenaica. Greek explorers and warriors had been visiting the region for hundreds of years—first as a passageway in an unsuccessful attempt to invade Egypt, and later as a plentiful fishing area. Eventually, the Greeks realized it was the only portion of North Africa that had not already been colonized and took greater control of the land. At first, the Greeks were welcomed by the people already living in Cyrenaica. It was a prosperous time in the region, with plenty of grains and fruits, as well as horses. But as more Greeks moved in to share the wealth, the local people began to rebel, sometimes successfully. Control of the land changed

The ruins of a Greek colony at Cyrenaica

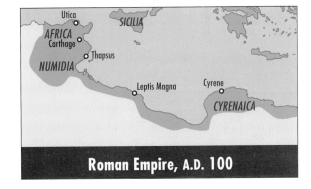

Roman Empire, A.D. 100

hands many times. Eventually, Cyrenaica, too, fell under Roman control.

The area's prosperity continued for several hundred years, and the population grew. Libya's largest city at the time was Leptis Magna, with approximately 80,000 citizens around A.D. 200. But as the Roman empire began to buckle, mostly under the weight of its own success, Romans lost control of North Africa.

The ruins of the Severan Basilica at Leptis Magna

After the Greeks and Romans came the Vandals, from the part of Northern Europe that is now Germany. They came to the region through Spain in about A.D. 435, attracted by North Africa's wealth. They were the first invaders to make serious attempts to settle some of Libya's mountain and desert areas. But the

Vandals, A.D. 450

nomadic tribes that lived in these regions often rebelled. The Vandals were conquered by Byzantium after about a century of rule. Arabs took over around A.D. 643.

Arabs in Libya

The Arab entry into Libya is a key point in the country's history because the Arabs brought the religion of Islam. When they arrived, Arabs and Islam were not well accepted, but over the centuries, both took strong hold. Within 400 years, most people in Libya were Muslims—followers of Islam. None of the Christian settlements established by the Greeks remained. Islam was not forced upon the people by the conquering Arabs, but they quickly adopted it because Islam's teachings about the equality of all men gave the people a way to justify their rebellion against conquerors. They wanted self-rule, and Islam gave them the courage to revolt.

Today 97 percent of Libya's people are Muslims, and the Arabic language is dominant throughout the country. Most Libyans today claim Arabic heritage. No other invading population played such a large role in shaping present-day Libya.

Preserving History

The Libyan government is working to preserve its rich historical sites and architecture, joining forces with the World Heritage Center to safeguard several sites. The World Heritage Center is part of the United Nations Educational, Scientific, and Cultural Organization (UNESCO). The center locates historical and cultural sites around the world that it feels should be preserved, and works to keep the sites from being damaged. It selected five cultural sites in Libya: Cyrene, Leptis Magna, Sabratha, Tadrart Acacus, and the ancient city of Ghadames.

- Cyrene, one of the most complex archaeological sites in the region, has a huge Roman amphitheater (left). It started out as a shrine to the Greek god Dionysus but was later enlarged by the Romans and turned into an arena where gladiators fought wild animals.
- Leptis Magna was one of the most beautiful cities in the Roman world. It is located on the coast, about 75 miles (120 km) east of Tripoli. Its architecture and construction were grand, including much marble and granite and ornately decorated walls and streets. But after being deserted for more than 1,000 years, the city was buried in sand. Most excavation work is completed, and while some of the monuments have been moved to museums, others have been restored on the site. In the late 1980s, a series of floods devastated the area, requiring more restoration work.

Ghadames (below) is a traditional settlement on an oasis in the desert—a walled city. Its clustered homes are made of clay and brick, and are whitewashed on the inside. Today, most residents have moved to more modern homes outside the city. With few inhabitants to keep the homes in good repair, the city is deteriorating rapidly. However, many residents of modern homes nearby also keep small homes in the old city where they live during the hot summer. Even though the modern homes have air conditioning, this "new" convenience cannot keep people as cool as the old clay houses whose thick walls hold the evening's coolness during the day.

- Sabratha, a port city, saw its greatest wealth during the second and third centuries A.D. Many monuments were built here. Among the most beautiful of these was a theater surrounded on three sides by walls of pink and white marble (above). During Italy's reign in Libya, Italian archaeologists worked to restore it, but the sea spray that blows onto it is damaging the marble. Located 37 miles (60 km) east of Tripoli, it is used today during the summer for cultural entertainment.

- Tadrart Acacus is located near Libya's southwest border, east of the city of Ghat. Here are cave paintings of animals, some dating back 12,000 years. But the site is not guarded, and the paintings are being destroyed. Damage has been caused by visitors and photographers who wet the drawings to make them stand out better, and by vandalism.

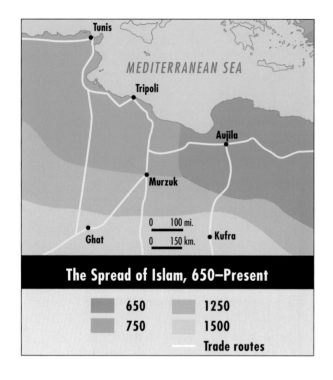

The Spread of Islam, 650–Present

650
750
1250
1500
Trade routes

The Arabs were not the last to take charge of the region, however. Norman Crusaders from Sicily captured Tripoli in 1146, and twelve years later, in 1158, a Muslim army from Morocco took control of the city. Over the next 200 years, these invaders, called the Almohads extended their reign to include almost all of Tripolitania. In 1510, a Spanish expedition sent to Tripoli by King Ferdinand captured the city. Spain held control until 1551, when the Ottoman Turks took over Tripoli and, eventually, the entire nation.

In taking control of Libya, the Ottomans had one thing in common with all those invaders over the centuries—they faced the opposition of the Libyan people. These were proud and stubborn people who refused to

The Sanusi Brotherhood

The Sanusi brotherhood, formed in 1837, was a religious group that played a large role in Libya's political history. Established as a return to the simple beliefs and lifestyle of early Islam, it was also a missionary order aimed at spreading Islam throughout the region.

The brotherhood's leader was known as the Grand Sanusi, and members pledged him their allegiance, both religious and political. They established lodges called *zawiyas* throughout Cyrenaica and in parts of Tripolitania,

as centers of local influence. They provided material assistance and spiritual and political guidance to members. The zawiyas became focal points for the resistance movements against several invaders—the French from the south during the Ottoman period, and then the Italian invaders.

Later, Sanusi leadership represented the Libyan people in negotiations with the Italians, and with the British after World War II. Libya's only king, Idris I, who ruled from 1951 to 1969, was the Grand Sanusi when he was made king.

Barbary Pirates

U.S. involvement in the Libyan region began during the late 1700s, when the United States fought for control of Mediterranean sea-lanes. The Barbary Pirates, named for the Berbers, sailed out of Tripoli to raid ships, including American merchant ships. They stole goods and took crew members as slaves. At one time, pirates held nearly 25,000 captives for ransom at spots along the Mediterranean coast. The pirates demanded money, called tribute, from nations before they would allow them to travel through the Mediterranean without being harassed.

Beginning in 1795, the United States paid the pirate leaders yearly fees of more than $2 million to keep them from attacking U.S. ships. In 1801, when the pirate leaders demanded even higher payments, the United States refused and fighting broke out. The United States created its navy to launch ships that put the pirates out of business. This origin is noted in the Marine Hymn, which begins, "From the halls of Montezuma to the shores of Tripoli. . . ."

The conflict ended with mixed results. The Barbary Pirates agreed to lower the tribute costs, and the United States continued to pay until 1815. After that, skirmishes with the pirates began anew and lasted for another fifteen years.

accept easily the colonial powers that tried to take over their land. They were helped by their harsh environment—Libyans knew better than any colonial people how to survive in Libya. Throughout history, groups of rebels continued to resist the invaders. Although the Ottoman Empire ruled Libyan territory for four centuries, eventually it too began to weaken.

When Italy's leaders saw that the Ottomans were losing their grip on Libya, they decided to move in. Italy wanted to colonize Libya for several reasons. Control of Tripoli would give Italy greater shipping powers in the Mediterranean Sea, and Italy also wanted a presence in Northern Africa. The British already controlled Egypt, and the Italians feared that

France wanted Libya. After months of fighting against the invading Italian forces, the Ottomans finally gave up their rights to Libya in 1911.

The Italian Invasion

When the Italians discovered the remains of beautiful cities built by their Roman ancestors centuries before, they declared that Libya was rightfully theirs. Soon, thousands of Italians moved into Libya and the Italian military made ferocious attempts to wipe out the Arabs. Death was the punishment of those who resisted. Hangings were common. Many who weren't killed were confined under horrible conditions in concentration camps. In several Arab settlements, the all-important community well was cemented over, forcing the people to either scatter in search of water or die. Herds of cattle were killed.

A few good things happened under Italian rule, though most were intended to help the Italian settlers. Roads were improved, and new irrigation systems delivered water to dry desert lands. Farm machinery was brought in to help produce more

A gathering at the amphi-theater in Carthage during Italian occupation, 1930

crops. Shipping ports saw improvements too. But because of the hardships imposed on the people, Libyans hated Italian rule. They pulled together a resistance army that, aided by Turks, almost defeated the Italian colonists during World War I (1914–1918). But following the war, Turkey was forced to leave Africa, and without its help, the Libyan resistance was unable to succeed.

After World War II, Libya was finally freed from Italian rule. During the war, battles were fought on Libya's

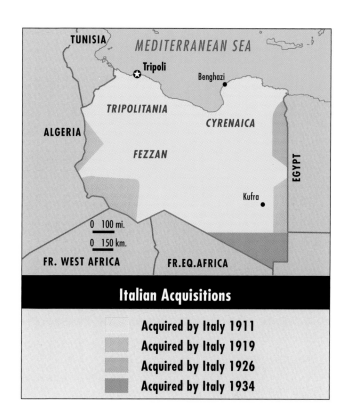

Italian Acquisitions

☐ Acquired by Italy 1911
▨ Acquired by Italy 1919
▨ Acquired by Italy 1926
▨ Acquired by Italy 1934

Omar Al-Mukhtar

It was a teacher, a scholar of the Qur'an, who led Libyans working secretly to overthrow the Italians. Their resistance group was called the *Mujahedeen* (Freedom Fighters). Omar Al-Mukhtar loved his studies, but he took action when Italian rule became intolerable. A leader in the Sanusi brotherhood, he organized a few hundred men in the city of Barqa and on the peaks of the Green Mountains, in northeast Libya.

With good horses but old military equipment, the resistance took on tens of thousands of Italian troops. These Libyans, strengthened by their love for their homeland, showed early success at holding back the Italian invaders, and their numbers grew to several thousand men and women from throughout Libya.

Al-Mukhtar became known as the Mentor of Bravery for his fearless leadership of the Mujahedeen. He was skilled at tracking the movements of his Italian enemies and used his great knowledge of Libya's landscape to ambush them, surprising them with forceful strikes.

By the time he was eighty years old, Al-Mukhtar had led the Mujahedeen for nearly twenty years. In 1931, he was wounded in battle and captured. The Italians shackled him in heavy chains, convicted him in a military trial, and hanged him in front of thousands of mourning Libyans on September 16, 1931. Al-Mukhtar is honored as one of Libya's greatest heroes. The story of his life was made into a movie, *The Lion of the Desert,* starring Anthony Quinn.

northern coast as the British, aided by the Libyan Arab Force, fought both Italy and Germany for control of North Africa. Libya was the site of several brutal battles, and Libyan cities changed hands many times. The fighting was fierce and many people died. In 1943, the Italians and Germans were defeated, and Libya was placed under the temporary rule of Great Britain and France. The United Nations was left to decide who should control Libya. As one of the founding nations of the United Nations, Great Britain had considerable influence. It was decided that Libya should become an independent constitutional monarchy. After centuries of foreign rule, Libya became an independent nation in 1951.

Finally Free

Mohammed Idris Al-Senussi was a leader of the Libyan resistance movement and had cooperated with the British forces to defeat the Italians. Idris became Libya's first king, chosen by a national assembly. His nation, called the United Kingdom of Libya, was made up of the three regional provinces, each led by a governor appointed by the king. Each governor was assisted by a council elected by the people.

King Idris

In return for the support he had received from Great Britain, and for financial and technical assistance he received from Great Britain and the United States, King Idris was helpful to these Western nations. He allowed them to establish military bases in Libya along the Mediterranean Sea, in order to keep the Soviet Union in check.

But even with help from Great Britain and the United States, the new nation had many problems. The three provinces, so long separated by history and geography, were used to working in their own best interests, not to working together for the good of the nation. As a result, there was little cooperation. Also, the country was racked by poverty. Farmland was limited following years of war, and modern technology was unheard of. In 1951, Libya was one of the poorest nations in the world.

King Idris imposed his own will on the people. He forced the leader of his opposition out of the country. Though he made improvements in the nation's health and educational systems, the lives of ordinary Libyan people really didn't get better. Only those among the king's favored group of people got rich. Even after the great oil fields were found in 1959 and money began to pour into the country, it stayed in the hands of that select few. Most Libyans lived the same impoverished lives they did before oil was discovered. Though more goods and services became available, the cost of living went up too.

King Idris ruled until 1969. By then, he was growing old and his government was increasingly corrupt. A group of Libyan army officers deposed—overthrew—him. The king fled to Egypt, and the young leader of the army officers took command of the country. His name was Muammar al-Qaddafi. As the twentieth century draws to a close, Qaddafi still leads the country.

Leading the Nation

Opposite: **Muammar al-Qaddafi**

M UAMMAR AL-QADDAFI WAS THE LEADER OF THE REBEL military group that ousted King Idris in 1969 in a swift *coup d'état,* or military takeover. Qaddafi and many others felt Idris was corrupt, and that he was allowing too many Western ideas to influence Libya.

Qaddafi (second from left) views a display of rockets in Yugoslavia.

While the king was away in Turkey for medical treatment, Qaddafi and his group seized the palace, took over the military bases, and locked up the king's supporters. Qaddafi then went on the radio and announced to the people of Libya that the government had been overthrown. At age twenty-seven, Qaddafi became leader of his nation.

Immediately, he made changes. He created an extensive web of leadership, with an executive, a legislative, and a judicial branch, much like the government of the United States. But Qaddafi's Libyan government has many more layers because he believes that this spreads the authority to more people.

Leading the Nation   **55**

The Boyhood Training of Qaddafi

When Muammar al-Qaddafi assumed leadership of Libya in September 1969, it was the culmination of preparation that had continued throughout his young life. Qaddafi was a Bedouin, a member of a nomadic tribe that raised small herds of goats and camels and moved frequently in search of food and water. They lived in homes made of goatskin stretched across sticks embedded in the sand. Because they rarely settled, it was difficult for nomads to establish a leadership role except among those with whom they traveled. Few leaders come from such a background.

But even at an early age, Qaddafi was different. He displayed an enormous intelligence, quickly picking up language. The young Qaddafi eagerly absorbed the Islamic teachings his family followed. He loved the traditions of prayer and religious study. His family recognized his unusual abilities and decided to make sacrifices in their lives in order to send their ten-year-old son to an Islamic boarding school in the coastal city of Surt.

Most of Qaddafi's classmates came from wealthy families in the modern cities along Libya's Mediterranean coast. Their fathers were businessmen, making money by dealing with Europeans and Americans following World War II. Most of these families were greatly influenced by Western traditions and values. Though they were Muslims, many of their traditional beliefs were being left behind.

Qaddafi was different, and not only because he was poor. Several of his ancestors died fighting the Italians and other foreigners who tried for centuries to control Libya. Qaddafi had no use for the Western traditions—the foods, clothing, and entertainment—that his classmates so enjoyed. He became a loner and immersed himself in his schoolwork, quickly rising to the top of his class.

To fill his lonely hours, he turned to a small transistor radio his family bought for him. He listened to Egyptian programs that featured speeches by Gamal Abdel Nasser, who was then president of Egypt. A favorite theme of Nasser's was his desire for Arab unity and political cooperation among the neighboring Arab nations, as well as rejection of Western ties. This was a philosophy young Qaddafi heartily embraced.

Qaddafi transferred to a secondary school in Sabha at age fourteen. This school was less exclusive and students included the sons of other poor families who were eager to hear Qaddafi's ideas. An energetic, serious boy with a strong personality, Qaddafi gathered around him a large but secretive group. They were already plotting the eventual overthrow of King Idris. These plans continued to grow and evolve as Qaddafi went on to the University of Libya, Libyan Military College, and then joined the Libyan Army.

On September 1, 1969, while King Idris was in Turkey, Qaddafi unleashed the plan he had been developing for more than ten years. Along with his secret group of supporters, Qaddafi stormed the royal palace and seized control of the nation. Though many wealthy, urban Libyans were upset with his government, Qaddafi received great support from the impoverished Bedouins.

Qaddafi's plans for Libya are based on three factors: economic and political freedom for the people of Libya; unity, both throughout Libya and with other nations in the Arab world; and Islamic law as the overall guide for justice.

The Green Book

Many governing principles of the country are expressed in Qaddafi's *Green Book*, so-titled because green is the color of Islam. In his book, Qaddafi describes his ideal political system, the Third Universal Theory. It is a government in which the people hold the power. He calls it a New Socialism, the goal of which is "to create a society that is happy because it is free." This can be achieved through satisfying the material and spiritual needs of humanity, states Qaddafi, and that, in turn, comes by obtaining these needs without outside control.

In 1970, General Numeiri of the Sudan, President Anwar el-Sadat of Egypt, and Muammar Qaddafi of Libya (left to right) united to form an Arab Federation.

Men and women are considered equal. The *Green Book* stresses the right and duty of Libyan women to participate in the nation's economy. At the same time, a woman's primary role is to be a good mother.

His government, asserts Qaddafi, is better than the "repugnant" capitalism and communism found in other parts of the world. Capitalism and communism have both failed, he declares, in their attempts to bring happiness to humanity. He named his philosophy the Third Universal Theory because it is, he believes, an alternative to capitalism and communism— a third and better way. The *Green Book*, Qaddafi writes, "presents the ultimate solution to the problem of the instrument of government."

Qaddafi believes that no government on Earth is truly a democracy in which the majority rules. It is, in fact, basically impossible for a true democracy to exist, for all people would have to vote on all issues facing the government—a system too time-consuming and complicated to implement. "The Third Universal Theory, however, now provides us with a practical approach to a direct democracy;" writes Qaddafi in the *Green Book*. "The problem of democracy in the world will finally be solved."

In 1977, Qaddafi gave his nation a new name: "The Socialist People's Libyan Arab Jamahiriya." Qaddafi created the term *jamahiriya*, meaning a republic of the masses— a place where all the people have a voice, and the ruling is done by the people. *Jamahiriya* is linguistically related to the Arabic term for republic.

Government of the People

Qaddafi and his team set up a complex process in which citizens could voice their opinions through smaller, local government bodies. There are 24 municipalities, called *baladiyat* in Arabic. Each of these is divided into a total of 186 zones. The citizens of each zone are grouped into their own Basic People's Congress. At the head of the country is Qaddafi, who

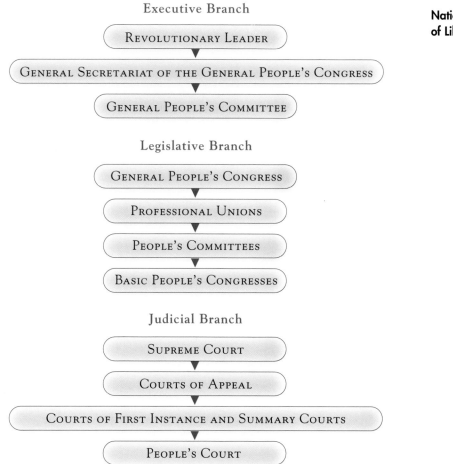

National Government of Libya

Executive Branch

REVOLUTIONARY LEADER

↓

GENERAL SECRETARIAT OF THE GENERAL PEOPLE'S CONGRESS

↓

GENERAL PEOPLE'S COMMITTEE

Legislative Branch

GENERAL PEOPLE'S CONGRESS

↓

PROFESSIONAL UNIONS

↓

PEOPLE'S COMMITTEES

↓

BASIC PEOPLE'S CONGRESSES

Judicial Branch

SUPREME COURT

↓

COURTS OF APPEAL

↓

COURTS OF FIRST INSTANCE AND SUMMARY COURTS

↓

PEOPLE'S COURT

holds the title of Revolutionary Leader. He is supported by the five members of the General Secretariat and the sixteen members of the General People's Committee.

Who's Really in Charge?

The democratic society that Qaddafi described is not the reality of life in Libya, however. By granting authority to hundreds

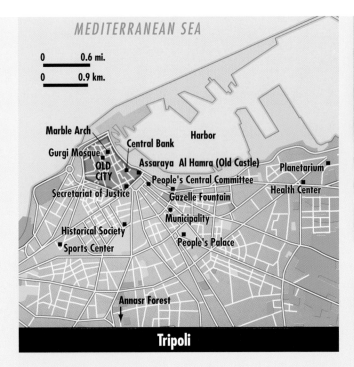

Tripoli

Tripoli: Did You Know This?

Population: 591,100 (1988)

Year founded: About 500 B.C.

Altitude: Sea level

Average Daily Temperature: 52°F (11.1°C) January; 81°F (27.2°C) July

Average Annual Rainfall: 16 inches (40 cm)

of small groups, he ensures that while each individual has a voice, there is no central power other than himself. Qaddafi lays down the law, supported by a military ready to defeat any challengers.

Qaddafi's government is based on Islamic principles. The nation's Constitution is the Islamic holy book, the Qur'an. The *shari'a*, or Islamic religious law, shapes the laws that govern daily life. Drinking alcohol and gambling are forbidden. Punishments that were listed in the Qur'an became the law: Break the fast of Ramadan, and be whipped; commit armed robbery, and you may lose an arm or a foot.

The Libyan Flag

Even the flag of Libya displays Qaddafi's fierce loyalty to Islam and his desire to unite Islam and Libya. The flag is a simple field of green, the color of Islam, unadorned by any symbols.

Although Islam itself calls for respect for both Jews and Christians, Qaddafi began persecuting people who followed other religions, especially Judaism and Christianity. Qaddafi led a movement to force Jews out of Libya, and much of their property was seized by the state. Most Christian churches were closed, and one Roman Catholic church was turned into an Islamic mosque.

Qaddafi later softened his views against other religions. In 1976, Libya sponsored a Muslim–Christian discussion in Tripoli, during which Qaddafi spoke of the need for greater understanding among Christians, Jews, and Muslims. However, less than 3 percent of Libya's people follow religions other than Islam today. Most of these people are Christians and Jews who have come to work in Libya.

Soldiers in training

At last count in August 1996, the Libyan military was made up of a 35,000-member army, an air force of 22,000, and 8,000 sailors in the navy. Large sums of money have been spent to ensure that Libya is a superpower among North African nations. In fact, the military owns more guns than its soldiers can use at any given time, and there is such a surplus of military tanks that many of them are simply lined up in the desert, rusting away. After centuries of colonization, Qaddafi is prepared to fight for Libya's continued independence at any time. He wants to make sure his country never again has to suffer the humiliation and anguish of rule by another nation.

Few Friends for Qaddafi

Though Qaddafi denies it, many world leaders believe that he supports terrorist activity—violent behavior—to achieve his goals. Over the last two decades, the United States has accused Libyans of bombing U.S. servicemen in Berlin and of shooting down a French passenger plane over Africa. The United States has also accused Libya of manufacturing poison gases that could be used in chemical warfare and of aiding terrorists from other countries who commit crimes against the United States.

In response to these alleged terrorist actions, the United States imposed sanctions on Libya beginning in 1982. These

restrictions and bans on trade were meant to damage Libya's economy, particularly its oil industry.

Further, the United States shot down two Libyan Air Force planes flying over the Mediterranean in 1981 and dropped bombs on Tripoli and Benghazi in 1986. These bombings, called for by then–U.S. president Ronald Reagan, were directed at sites believed to be centers of terrorism. Qaddafi had a home in one of these areas, and it was bombed. Dozens of Libyan civilians and soldiers were killed along with, according to some reports, Qaddafi's infant daughter. Two of Qaddafi's sons, ages three and four, were injured in the attack.

Polls taken after the bombing of Libya showed that while most Americans approved of the action, many citizens of other nations did not approve—particularly Europeans and Arabs. Sympathy for Libya increased worldwide. But within a few years, Westerners again questioned Qaddafi's role in terrorist activity.

Pan American Flight 103

On December 21, 1988, Pan American Flight 103 left Frankfurt, Germany, carrying 259 people. The plane never reached its New York destination. Instead, it blew up over Lockerbie, Scotland, killing everyone on board, including 189 Americans, and 11 people on the ground. It took more than two years for investigators to uncover the cause of the explosion. They found a small computer chip among the rubble that they believe tied the crash to two Libyan intelligence officers. In November 1991, a U.S. court charged the two Libyans, Abdel Basset Ali Megrahi and Lamen Khalifa Fhimah, with planting a bomb on the plane.

Libya denied any responsibility for the bombing and refused to turn over the two suspects to the United States or Great Britain, arguing that the men could never get a fair trial in either country. Neither side would give in. In an attempt to pressure Qaddafi to change his mind, the United Nations voted to impose sanctions on the country. In 1992, the UN banned air travel to and from Libya, prohibited the sale of military weaponry to Libya, and limited the sale of equipment used in the oil industry. These were in addition to the trade sanctions already placed by the United States.

Unfortunately, most economic experts agree that the sanctions mainly hurt ordinary Libyans, particularly their health care. The country was unable to get up-to-date medicines and treatments and was also unable to fly critically ill patients out of the country for better treatment elsewhere. However, until recently, the sanctions seem to have had little or no effect on Qaddafi.

In April 1999, Libya turned over the suspects on the condition that a trial take place on neutral grounds. It will be held in the Netherlands under Scottish law. The two suspects have declared themselves innocent, but could face life imprisonment if they are convicted. They are charged with murder, conspiracy to commit murder, and violations of international aviation safety laws. The sanctions previously imposed by the UN were suspended the day Megrahi and Fhimah were turned over.

What's Qaddafi Really Like?

Is Qaddafi a "madman," as a few have labeled him? Some people think so, because of the intense hatred he has expressed toward Western lifestyles and governments. But others point out that Qaddafi is really no "worse" than several other Middle Eastern leaders whose countries have not been subject to as much punishment as Libya from the United States and other powerful Western nations. Some scholars suggest that Qaddafi angers Western leaders so much because he refuses to act like an underdog—Qaddafi remains firm in his beliefs and stands strong in his actions.

Now there are new questions. U.S. officials have recently been concerned about Qaddafi's Great Man-Made River.

Qaddafi gives a speech at the inauguration of the Great Man-Made River project.

Foreign engineers working on the project said in December 1997 that the underground tunnels are so large that it is not realistic to believe they will be used only for water. More likely, they say, Qaddafi plans to use the extensive underground network to store and move military equipment and troops without being detected.

Libya has had poor relations with most of its neighboring countries too. It was involved in a border war with Chad for more than twenty years, and there have been tensions with other North African and Arab nations, including Egypt, Morocco, Sudan, Tunisia, and Syria. Qaddafi has tried to form unions with all these countries, but none has worked out. Qaddafi is also suspected of having a role in political upheavals in Burkina Faso and Sierra Leone. But some people feel that Qaddafi gets blamed for much of the trouble throughout the Arab world because he is an easy target.

Former South African president Nelson Mandela made a show of friendship with Qaddafi. Libya backed Mandela and his struggle against apartheid in South Africa, and Mandela visited Libya twice in late 1997. He awarded Qaddafi South Africa's highest award for a foreigner, the Order of Good Hope. In June 1999, Qaddafi traveled to Pretoria, South Africa, for the inauguration of Thabo Mbeki, Mandela's successor as president of South Africa.

South African President Nelson Mandela (left) showed his support for Libya outside of Qaddafi's bombed home in 1997.

Whether Qaddafi is friend or foe, crazy or sane, a troublemaker or a peacemaker depends on whom you ask. Even among his fellow Libyans, there is disagreement.

Qaddafi is adored by some Libyan citizens, hated by others. He got much of his original support from citizens whose lives improved after he took over. The money that was pouring into the country from oil exports was used to better the lives of ordinary citizens through new schools, better hospitals, and improved roadways. Almost everyone in the country had an easier life and more money to spend. While King Idris was in power, most of the oil money had stayed in the hands of a few wealthy citizens. Qaddafi saw that it was spread around, and of course, the people liked that.

But in recent years, oil prices around the world have gone down, so less money is flowing into Libya now. And some Libyans are growing tired of Qaddafi's refusal to accept any ideas that differ from his own. Still, though he has often faced opposition during his years in power, Qaddafi has no obvious rival to his leadership of Libya.

The quality of life has increased for some Libyans because Qaddafi has redistributed the wealth.

As long as Libya's economy is healthy, Qaddafi will likely continue to have the support of most Libyans. But if the country's economy, so dependent on oil, begins to suffer serious problems, Qaddafi will probably have problems too.

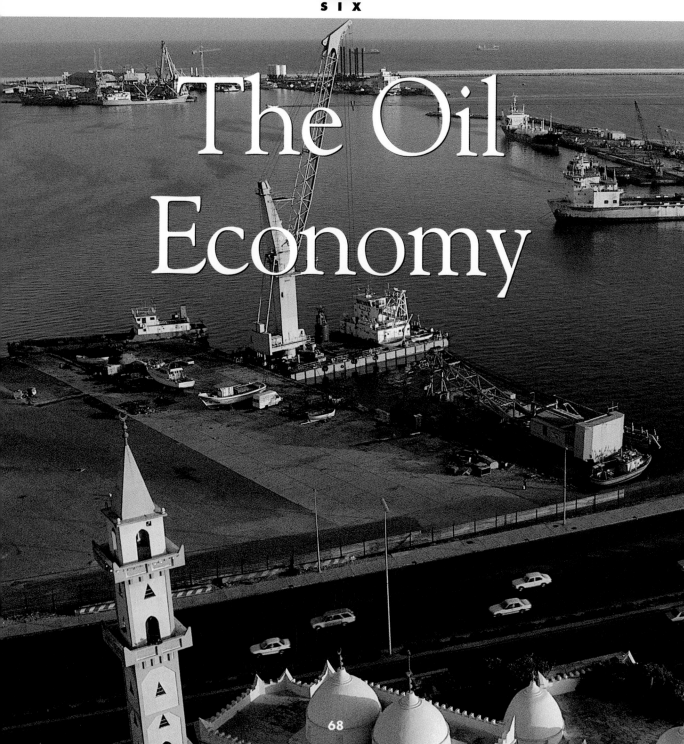

The Oil Economy

LIBYA'S INCOME IS BASED SOLIDLY UPON THE OIL FLOWING under its desert. When there is a great demand for oil and prices are high, Libya's economy generally does well. But when oil prices begin to drop, as they have in recent years when the worldwide demand for oil lessened, Libya's economy shows signs of trouble too.

Libya has been one of Africa's wealthiest nations ever since the discovery of oil in 1959. Prior to that, it was among the world's poorest nations, dependent upon aid from the United States and Great Britain. The only work was found on farms and in a few factories.

A horse cart transporting kitchen appliances

With oil profits, all that changed. Demand for Libya's crude oil was high. It contained less sulfur than oil from other parts of the world, so it was easier, cheaper, and cleaner to use. Foreign aid was no longer necessary. The country had plenty of money to spend on its own

Libyan women working at a TV factory

infrastructure—building roads, schools, hospitals, and strengthening the military. During the 1970s, Libya's power plants produced seven times more electricity to meet the growing need. New apartments were built for low-income citizens, and programs to help the poor were improved. Thousands of jobs were created.

Many Libyans earned good wages working in the oil industry. They wanted to spend their money on modern luxuries, such as kitchen appliances and television sets. The demand for these products went up, and more people got jobs making

The Dinar

The monetary unit in Libya is the dinar, and 1 dinar contains 1,000 dirhams. In 1985, one dinar was equal to about U.S.$3.38. By 1999, the dinar had dropped in value and was equal to about U.S.$2.22. The sanctions that restricted trade with Libya caused much of the drop, making Libyan currency less valuable on the world market.

Libyan coins display the Libyan coat of arms. The coat of arms features a hawk, carrying in its feet a banner with the country's name in Arabic. In front of the hawk is a shield of green, the color of Islam and of Libya's flag. The prophet Muhammad, who founded the Islamic religion, belonged to the Quraish tribe. The hawk was the tribe's symbol.

Symbols on Libya's paper money vary with the denomination. The 1-dinar bills, for example, feature a portrait of Qaddafi on the front and a mosque on the back.

them. Shops sprang up to sell the merchandise. Many of these workers wanted better homes, so there were more jobs available in the building industry too. The oil money brought great improvements throughout Libya's economy. But there are cracks showing in the strong economy.

Too Many in Charge

Part of Qaddafi's plans for the Jamahiriya called for the end of workers earning wages from an employer. Instead, workers would become associates, taking home equal portions of the

The Souk

In Libya, the heart of the retail industry is the *souk*. Souks are lively, colorful outdoor markets found in most cities. Here, farmers sell their crops, merchants sell spices and all sorts of other goods, and craftspeople sell their works, such as jewelry and metal engravings. Some craftspeople even work at their stalls in the souk, creating baskets, rugs, and decorative pieces with metals and leather.

profits. Qaddafi's reason for this is found in the *Green Book*: "Wage-earners are but slaves to the masters who hire them." To free Libya from this type of "slavery," stores and factories were put into the hands of the workers, all of whom shared leadership. "In this society," writes Qaddafi, "there are no wage-earners, but partners."

This system soon bogged down, with no one in charge to make business decisions. When everything had to be voted on by everybody, business moved as slowly as a tired camel.

Then the government got even more involved, adding many regulations to most businesses. This slowed things down to the point where the economy was almost at a standstill, buried under the weight of too many leaders and too much red tape. Finally, Qaddafi relaxed the regulations and allowed some businesses to be owned by a single individual. The economy has only partially recovered, however. The government still owns all the hotels and soft-drink bars. There are no taverns or liquor stores in Libya because alcohol is banned.

There is an increasing demand for luxury items since the oil industry improved the economy.

It Doesn't Pay to Save

In the *Green Book*, Qaddafi states that large sums of money are saved only at the expense of others, and that no person should save more than is needed. "Any surplus beyond the satisfaction of needs should ultimately belong to all members of society," he writes, adding that those who "acquire excessively," are "undoubtedly thieves."

During his early years in power, Qaddafi tried to make people give up most of their savings. His attempts were unsuccessful because people simply hid their savings in their homes. So in the 1980s, Qaddafi changed the type of money used in Libya. Everyone had to turn in their old money in exchange for the new money. Anyone who turned in more than the equivalent of U.S.$2,100 in old money received only the equivalent of U.S.$2,100 in the new money, and was given a receipt for the rest. The receipt has proven to be worthless. Qaddafi used the extra money to provide more products and services for the poor. This improved the lives of the poor, but it infuriated the people who had earned the money. They lost their motivation to work harder and earn more. This lack of motivation has taken another toll on Libya's economy.

Men working in the oil fields

Sanctions Cause Problems

The economic sanctions placed on Libya by the United Nations after the Pan Am Flight 103 bombing were another major problem. UN member nations were urged not to trade with Libya. This caused great difficulties for Libya, which needs to import food and many other products, and wants to export its main product—oil. Several countries do still buy their oil from Libya, however. Italy and Germany are Libya's main trading partners today.

The worldwide drop in oil demand and price caused wages in Libya to drop by about 25 percent during the 1980s. There were some signs that wages and income were on the rise again during the 1990s. Now that the two accused terrorists have been turned over for trial and the UN sanctions have been lifted, the Libyan economy is likely to improve.

In any case, the oil won't be around much longer. Libya's oil deposits are predicted to be used up by about the year 2015.

Planning for the Future

Plans are being made for the end of the oil boom. Qaddafi expects the Great Man-Made River to do wonders for the agricultural sector, enabling the country to grow enough food

Irrigation systems in the Kafra Desert

for its own people and to export food as well. Already, construction of the vast underground tunnel system has created thousands of jobs, though many of them have gone to foreigners. But will it really work? No one knows for sure. Many experts feel that it will cost more to pump the water to the agricultural centers than to buy the food from another country. And of course, just as the oil will run out, the underground reservoirs that provide the water are predicted to run dry in about fifty years.

At that time, Libya may be forced to return to its old economic system. Though this sector of the economy has been overshadowed by the huge oil profits, the old ways still exist. The traditional economy was based primarily on agriculture,

Some large oases are suitable for growing crops.

with a few factories. But even with the agricultural trade, the country must import 75 percent of its food. Only a few large oases and the thin strip of land along the Mediterranean coast are suitable for farming. Much of that coastal land is used for other purposes too. Housing and urban development take up a large chunk—90 percent of all Libya's citizens live along the coast. Seaports and the shipping industry also take up space. As a result, only about 1 percent of Libya's total land is cultivated.

Libyan Agriculture

The major crops grown in Libya are cereals, such as barley and wheat. Some farmers have groves of olive trees, and others have orchards of almonds, watermelons, citrus fruits, dates,

What Libya Grows, Makes, and Mines

Agriculture (1996)

Watermelons	180,000 metric tons
Wheat	168,000 metric tons
Barley	150,000 metric tons

Manufacturing (1995)

Residual fuel oils (est.)	5,100,000 metric tons
Distillate fuel	4,200,000 metric tons
Cement (est.)	2,300,000 metric tons

Mining

Crude petroleum (1996)	525,600,000 barrels
Natural gas (1996)	6,200,000,000 cubic meters
Gypsum (1995, est.)	160,000 metric tons

A sheep farmer near
Benghazi

Men fishing with nets

apricots, and figs. Peanuts, tomatoes, grapes, tobacco, and beans are also grown.

Raising cattle is another important segment of agriculture in parts of Libya, particularly Cyrenaica. Grazing lands in the region are jointly owned by a group of several farmers. Libya has about 4.4 million sheep, 800,000 goats, 120,000 camels, and 50,000 head of cattle. While the camels are used mostly for transportation—they are still the most dependable way to cross the desert—the other animals mainly provide milk, meat, and hides. A few poultry farms, with about 15 million birds, are also springing up. Other animals include mules, horses, and donkeys.

Fish is not in great demand in Libya, even though the country borders the sea. A few people fish commercially off the shores of Tripolitania, catching mostly tuna and sardines.

A Small Manufacturing Segment

Some people work in factories. Most factories are in Tripoli and Benghazi, and they are usually small, with 100 workers or less. Here, workers produce processed food, tobacco, salt, fabrics, leather goods, cement, and beverages. Other factories produce items for the oil industry, such as tanks, steel drums, and pipe fittings.

As the demand for oil has dropped, so has the need to manufacture oil-related products. It seems unlikely that Libya's economy will ever return to its heyday. But even though the economic ropes have tightened, most experts agree that the wealth in Libya is distributed more equally than it is in most other developing countries.

The fabric-printing room of the Gazour textile complex in Tripoli

A People United

Opposite: **A Libyan woman soldier**

LIBYA IS CONSIDERED PART OF THE ARAB WORLD—MOST OF its citizens are Arabs. Additional African nations of the Arab world include Morocco, Algeria, Tunisia, and Egypt. Arabs also live in Mauritania, the Sudan, and Western Sahara, which is now claimed by Morocco. The remaining eleven Arab countries, on the Arabian Peninsula and to the north, are Saudi Arabia, the United Arab Emirates, Qatar, Oman, Yemen, Lebanon, Syria, Jordan, Iraq, Kuwait, and Bahrain.

Together, the countries of the Arab world represent about 160 million people sharing the same language—Arabic—and similar cultures. But there are differences too. Some Arabs are Christians and a few are Jews, but most are Muslims. Some are dark-skinned and some are light-skinned. The history and economy of each country influences the way its citizens live.

In Libya, people's lives—their activities, their plans, and even their hopes—reflect several things

Libyan children in Wadi Ajal

in their long history. These include centuries of oppression and rule by other countries, generations of poverty turned suddenly to wealth, a nomadic ancestry, and a leader who is determined to keep out Western influence.

The People of Libya

More than 5.6 million people live in Libya, with the greatest numbers of people clustered around the port cities of Tripoli, the capital, with a population of about 591,000, and Benghazi, population 446,250.

A Growing Population

Libya's rate of population growth is one of the fastest among all African nations. Its population grows by nearly 4 percent annually. Some of this increase is due to the large number of foreigners that come to work in Libya. But it is also due to the nation's vast improvements in health care since oil money started flowing in. Between 1970 and 1985, the number of doctors grew to seven times what it had been, and the number of hospital beds tripled. However, Libya still has one of North Africa's highest rates of infant mortality—the number of children who die at birth or in infancy. Even so, nearly half of Libya's citizens are 15 years old or younger.

Most Libyan citizens—more than 90 percent—are Arabic-speaking Sunni Muslims of mixed Arabic and Berber ancestry. The other 10 percent of the people include members of the Tuareg tribes, Berbers, black Africans, and some people of Greek origin.

A number of foreign workers also live in Libya. Most came from other Arab nations to work in the oil fields and on the Great Man-Made River. Other well-educated workers came to Libya from Europe. People from more than 100 nations live in Libya.

Who Lives in Libya? (1995)

Arabs and Berbers	79%
Other (black Africans, Chadians, Egyptians, Greeks, Indians, Maltese, Italians, Pakistanis, Sudanese, Tebou, Tuareg, Tunisians, Turks)	21%

Old City in Tripoli

A People United   **83**

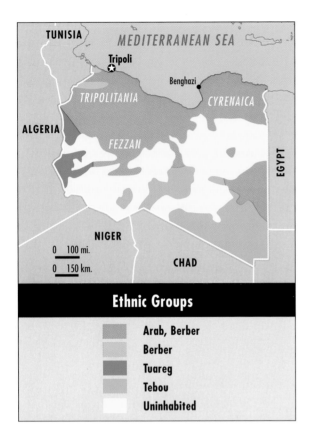

This sign in Arabic begins, "Eternal life and glory for the Arab nations. . . ."

The Arabic Language

Arabic is the official language of Libya, but English is sometimes used in government and business, as well as in science, technology, and medicine. Sometimes Italian and French are heard, along with some dialects from the nomadic tribes of the Sahara.

Arabic is read from right to left, in contrast to English and many other languages that are read from left to right. Spoken by more than 150 million people, mainly in North Africa, the Middle East, and Asia, Arabic is a lyrical language. Written Arabic is also pretty to look at with graceful, flowing strokes.

Nomads at the Start

The ancestors of most Libyans were members of nomadic tribes, and some Libyans still follow that ancient way of life. There is rarely extra food—usually just enough to live on. The weather is demanding—burning hot and freezing cold. Nothing comes easy in the desert, but people have lived this way in Libya's Sahara for thousands of years.

Though their life seems isolated, nomads are sociable people. They usually travel in groups, and strangers who come

The Arabic–English Connection

Several words in the English language are taken from similar Arabic words, such as algebra, almanac, artichoke, cotton, traffic, lemon, magazine, mattress, orange, satin, spinach, and syrup. Here are a few Arabic phrases:

Asalaam-o-Aleikum (ah-sah-LAY-moo ah-LAY-kuhm)   Peace be with you
(formal greeting)

Aleikum-o-Asalaam (ah-LAY-kuh-moo sah-LAHM)   Peace be with you
(polite reply)

Shoukran (SHUHK-rahn)   Thank you

And some numbers:

wahid	one
ithnayn	two
thalatha	three
arba	four
khamsa	five

A nomad woman of the Sahara

Nomad women in colorful traditional clothes

upon their campsites are greeted warmly. Nomads know that to turn people out into the desert alone will likely cause their death, so instead, they feed the strangers and care for them for a traditional period of three days.

Nomads travel with their cattle so no area is overgrazed. In this way, they preserve the fragile desert environment. Some nomads have settled in oases, and today the nomadic lifestyle is becoming a thing of the past. Still, some remain. The most well-known tribes in Libya are the Berbers, the Bedouin, and the Tuareg.

The Berbers

The Berbers once inhabited most of North Africa, but today, although many Libyans have some Berber ancestry, true Berbers make up only about 3 percent of Libya's population. The Berbers were not always nomadic. They lived in small tribes along the coast and farmed for a living until modern civilization pushed them out. Most have moved to the Jabal Nafusah highlands near Tripoli, where they remain isolated. In order to feed their goats and sheep, they live a partially nomadic life, sometimes herding the animals great distances to find water.

Most Berbers are tall people with light complexions. They usually speak the traditional Berber language, but most are also fluent in Arabic. They identify closely with members of their individual tribes rather than with all Berbers. Most are Muslim, but they practice a less strict form of the religion than urban Muslims. They have kept some of their religious traditions and honor their own saints and holy places.

The Bedouin

The Bedouin are Arabs belonging to several nomadic tribes. Qaddafi is a Bedouin. The word *bedouin* means "those who live in the desert." And this they do. Many are nomadic herders who travel with their horses and camels, carrying their tents and all their possessions with them. Other Bedouins have set up small farming communities near oases. These are the home base for the young men who follow the herds in search of water. The Bedouin tribes came to Libya in the eleventh century.

A Tuareg man wearing the characteristic veil and blue cotton clothing

The Tuareg

Tuareg people are known by the distinctive indigo blue cotton clothing many of them wear. In an unusual twist, it is the Tuareg men who cover their faces with veils, not the women. Many people believe this is for protection from the blowing sand, but wearing the veil is actually a social

Population of Major Cities (1988 estimate)	
Tripoli	591,100
Benghazi	446,250
Misratah	121,700
Az-Zawiyah	89,338

custom. The men often keep their faces uncovered while traveling but put on the veil in the presence of strangers and those of higher social class.

Tuareg families live in portable tents made of leather. They raise livestock—mostly goats and sheep—and travel with their goods on camels. Camel milk is one of their main foods. Traditionally, the Tuareg were desert couriers, carrying goods across the sands from one region to another. Today, with transport provided by trucks and planes, there are fewer truly nomadic Tuareg. Their numbers have also gone down since severe droughts struck the Sahel—the region surrounding the Sahara where some foods can be grown—in the 1970s and 1980s. Many Tuareg died, but a few Tuareg remain in Libya today to carry on the ancient traditions.

Apartments in Benghazi

A Move to the City

Most Libyans live in cities. They've given up nomadic life, life in an oasis village, or farming. This shift from a rural life to an urban one took place from the 1950s through the 1970s, following the economic boom that came with the discovery of oil. Libyans found it easier to live in cities, where jobs were more plentiful and wages were fairly good and predictable.

After Qaddafi took over, his government made a special effort to encourage rural people to move to larger cities. It is easier for the government to provide services, such as education and health care, to citizens living close together. It is also easier to organize people into political groups, something that is important to Qaddafi's Jamahiriya. As the nomads and rural people settled into cities, their traditional chains of authority and leadership were broken along with their traditional lifestyles. This gave Qaddafi's government a greater opportunity for control. Today, more than 75 percent of Libyans live in urban areas.

Population density—the number of people living in a certain size area—averages about 80 people per square mile (31 per sq km) in the two northern regions of Tripolitania and Cyrenaica, but falls to only 1.6 people per square mile (less than 1 person per sq km) in Libya's desert regions. Ninety percent of the people of Libya live on 10 percent of the land.

A busy Tripoli street

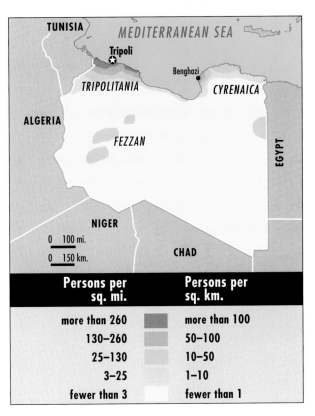

Population distribution in Libya

Persons per sq. mi.		Persons per sq. km.
more than 260		more than 100
130–260		50–100
25–130		10–50
3–25		1–10
fewer than 3		fewer than 1

A Prophet Leaves His Mark

AS IN THE REST OF THE ARAB WORLD, MOST PEOPLE IN Libya—97 percent—are Muslims, followers of Islam. A small number of people are Roman Catholics and Jews.

The Islamic Faith

Islam was founded around A.D. 610 by the prophet Muhammad. Muhammad was born forty years earlier in the city of Mecca, which is now in the country of Saudi Arabia. Muhammad felt a special calling from God, called *Allah* in Arabic, and soon had a vision of the Angel Gabriel. Gabriel told Muhammad about the "Word of God," explaining how people should live, what they should believe, and the way they should worship.

The word *Islam,* in Arabic, means "peace, purity, and sub-mission [to God]," and *Muslim* means "one who submits." Muhammad submitted to his duty and began to share his

Followers of Religions in Libya (1992)

Sunni Muslims	97%
Other Muslims, Christians, Jews	3%

The Qur'an

A Prophet Leaves His Mark **91**

vision. Eventually it was written down in the Qur'an (sometimes spelled Koran)—Islam's holy book, which Muslims believe records the exact words of God. *Qur'an* is an Arabic word meaning "recitation."

Allah is the same God that Christians and Jews worship. Many of the Qur'an's writings are similar to those found in the Old Testament of the Bible, and all the prophets of Judaism and Christianity are respected in the Islamic religion. Muslims believe that Jesus Christ was a great teacher and prophet, but they do not believe that he was the son of God, as Christians do. Muslims also believe in final judgment for humans: heaven for good people, and hell for those who have been evil. Muslims accept the existence of guardian angels.

Muhammad Faces Troubles

Few people listened to Muhammad at first. Most already followed their own religion. In Libya, religious beliefs dated back hundreds of years. When the Carthaginians ruled the land, their strong faith influenced Libyan religion. They believed in many gods with great powers. Christianity, introduced by Egyptians, was also a popular faith in the eastern part of Libya.

Muhammad's teachings angered the wealthy, powerful people in Mecca. They particularly despised Muhammad's statement that Allah was the one great power, and his order to share riches with the poor. When his life was threatened, Muhammad knew he had to leave Mecca. So in the year 622, he began his journey north, to Medina.

This journey—the *Hejira*—gave Muhammad an opportunity to preach to a group of people who were more willing to accept his ideas. It was an important time in the Islamic religion, when many people turned to the faith. In 630, Muhammad and his followers returned to Mecca and reestablished it as a holy city.

Muhammad died in 632, but Islam continued to spread. Traders carried their new faith with them along with their goods. More important, Arab soldiers who were followers of Islam conquered other countries. The Arab soldiers—called Moors in North Africa—called their holy war a *jihad*. Residents of the conquered lands became Muslims too, and in less than 100 years the Islamic Empire stretched from Spain in the west to Afghanistan in the east.

A woodcut of the Temple of Mecca, 1850s

A Prophet Leaves His Mark **93**

The Sanusi Movement

Islam grew even stronger in Libya after 1837, when a man named Sidi Muhammad ibn-Ali al-Sanusi took to preaching to the Muslims of Libya. He stressed the need to return to the traditional teachings of the Qur'an and the fundamental beliefs of Muhammad. He became known as the Grand Sanusi, and gained many followers. He also sent teachers, called *sheikhs*, to live among the small communities scattered throughout Libya.

The sheikhs instructed the people to build *zawiyas*, lodges that became central to the community. Each sheikh reigned as the community's absolute ruler—administrator, judge, and spiritual leader. Because each community throughout rural Libya had its own sheikh, several of these groups developed their own unique ways of following the teachings of Muhammad.

Islam in Libya through History

Most followers of Islam, including those in Libya, are Sunni Muslims, while the others are Shiites. The main split involves disagreement over who was the true successor to Muhammad as the ruler of Islam, in a position known as the *Caliph,* or prophet's deputy. These groups are divided further into about 800 various branches.

Even in Libya, there are factions of the Islamic faith. In parts of Fezzan and Cyrenaica, there is still some influence of the Sanusi brotherhood. The Sanusi were a group of Libyan Muslims founded in 1842 that followed strict Islamic law,

preaching morality and pure thoughts. Their teachings were popular with the nomadic Berber tribes, and the Sanusi movement spread into Tripolitania and Fezzan. The Sanusi were powerful political as well as spiritual leaders, and although Qaddafi has banned the brotherhood, memories of it linger with many older Libyans.

Another group are the sharifs who originated in Fezzan. Sharifs are individuals who claim to be direct descendants of Muhammad, and are therefore highly respected. They are believed to be holy men possessed with the power from God to see the future. Many oases in western Libya are controlled by sharifs.

Marabouts are another group of holy men who now live mostly in western Libya. The term *marabout* was first used to mean a Muslim holy man. In North Africa, it later came to mean a Muslim missionary and then, a Sufi leader. Marabouts give up the comforts of normal society and own only the bare necessities of life. Marabouts often dance and spin about wildly while chanting prayers in order to reach a trancelike or ecstatic state. They believe this brings them closer to God. Marabouts are said to have supernatural powers, called *baraka*. They usually live alone as hermits, but in a few rural regions they are accepted by the local residents and have settled in. It is believed that a marabout's baraka remains in his tomb after death, so their tombs are considered spiritual places by the community.

Sufism is a form of Islam that focuses more on the mystical side of religion than on the strict rules and regulations of the

Islamic faith. It is very personal and emotional, and its followers, too, choose to live alone and without comforts. During the eighteenth and nineteenth centuries, sufis formed brotherhoods, or associations, and were very influential in Libya. These religious brotherhoods helped resist the spread of Christianity across Libya by missionaries.

Important Religious Holidays

The following religious holidays are based on the Muslim lunar calendar and fall on different dates and in different months according to the Gregorian calendar used by many nations.

Ras al-Sanah al-Hijriya (First day of Muharram—Islamic New Year)
Eid al-Fitr (End of Ramadan)
Eid al-Adha (Feast of the Sacrifice)

Islam Continues to Grow

Today, more than 1 billion Muslims live throughout the world, and the number continues to grow. Most live in Africa, the Middle East, and Asia, but many people in the United States and Canada, particularly young African-Americans, are turning to Islam.

A line of coffins travels toward the Al Hani Mosque in Tripoli for a martyr's burial.

The Five Pillars of Islam

The Five Pillars of Islam are rules that make up the backbone of the Islamic religion.

1. **Shahada** is a statement of faith: "There is no god but Allah; Muhammad is his Prophet."
2. **Salat** is prayer. Muslims pray five times a day—at dawn, noon, mid-afternoon, dusk, and after dark, facing Mecca each time.
3. **Zakat** is giving alms. Muslims should give generously to the poor.
4. **Sawm** is fasting, or going without food. Muslims fast during Ramadan, the ninth month of the Muslim calendar.
5. The **Hajj** is a pilgrimage. Muslims make a pilgrimage to Mecca at least once, if possible.

Islam requires its followers to pay close attention to its rules, especially the Five Pillars of Islam; to pray frequently; and to take their faith seriously. The religion strongly influences the lifestyle of most Muslims. Muslim leaders study the Qur'an to determine the precise practices that Muslims must follow. In this way, the leaders have a role similar to judges.

Prayer is central to the lives of Muslims—they must pray five times daily—and the mosque, their house of worship, is central to each city or village. Traditionally, Muslims were called to the mosque by a muezzin, a man who stood in the minaret, a tower near the entrance of the mosque. In modern times, especially in cities, the call to prayer is often prerecorded and played through loudspeakers.

When people enter the mosque, they remove their shoes and wash their feet, hands, and faces. A certain spot in the mosque is reserved for women, but they usually stay home to worship. Mosques have central courtyards for prayer. Muslims pray facing Mecca, indicated inside the mosque by a *mihrab*—a small niche on the wall. The prayer leader is known as the *imam*. Muslims must pray at the mosque on Fridays, but many pray there at other times too.

Worshippers gather around the Kabah in Mecca.

At some point during their lives, all Muslims who can afford it are required to make a pilgrimage to the holy city of Mecca. Each year there is a special time for this pilgrimage, known as the *Hajj*. In Mecca, Muslims visit their holiest shrine, a cube-shaped building called the *Kabah*, and perform various rituals. The pilgrimage is completed on the most important Muslim holiday, *Eid al-Adha* (Feast of the Sacrifice). An animal—usually a goat or sheep—is sacrificed, and the meat is given to the poor. This sacrifice has deep religious significance. After completing this pilgrimage, a person may use the term *al-Haj* (for men) or *al-Hajja* (for women) before his or her name, a great honor.

Muslim men praying at Mecca

Opposite: **The major mosque in Tripoli**

In addition to the Five Pillars of Islam, other rules must be followed. For instance, Muslims must not drink liquor, gamble, or commit adultery. They may not eat pork or any other meat still containing blood. When lending money to others, they may not charge unusually high rates of interest. They must, in general, be respectful toward all, treating others with honesty, generosity, and fairness.

Islam in Libya Today

Because of the work of the Grand Sanusi and the sheiks who spread the teachings of the Qur'an, Islam became central to both communities and individual people throughout Libya. This continues to be true today.

The laws of Islam are a part of Libyan law. In Canada and the United States, religion and government are kept separate, but not in Libya. All laws must conform to Islamic religious law, called *Sharia*. A devout Muslim himself, Qaddafi has said he intends to restore Islam to its proper place in society. Libya is among the strictest of all Muslim countries, and religious holidays and practices are strictly observed there.

Yet while Qaddafi maintains that Islam is the perfect religion, he has shown tolerance for other religious views in Libya. For example, though there are few Jews in Libya, Qaddafi has recently rebuilt the Great Synagogue—a Jewish house of worship—and a Jewish school as part of a rehabilitation program in Tripoli. Both had been damaged after he seized power. Most of the 30,000 Jews in Libya left at that time, when their property was taken over by the government.

In the late 1990s, Qaddafi issued a statement that "we respect all places of worship," and invited Jews who had left "to come home." Qaddafi considers Christians to be misguided Muslims who have strayed from the true path of Islam by their belief that Jesus is the son of God.

An image of Qaddafi is surrounded by Libyan flags displayed in front of a mosque.

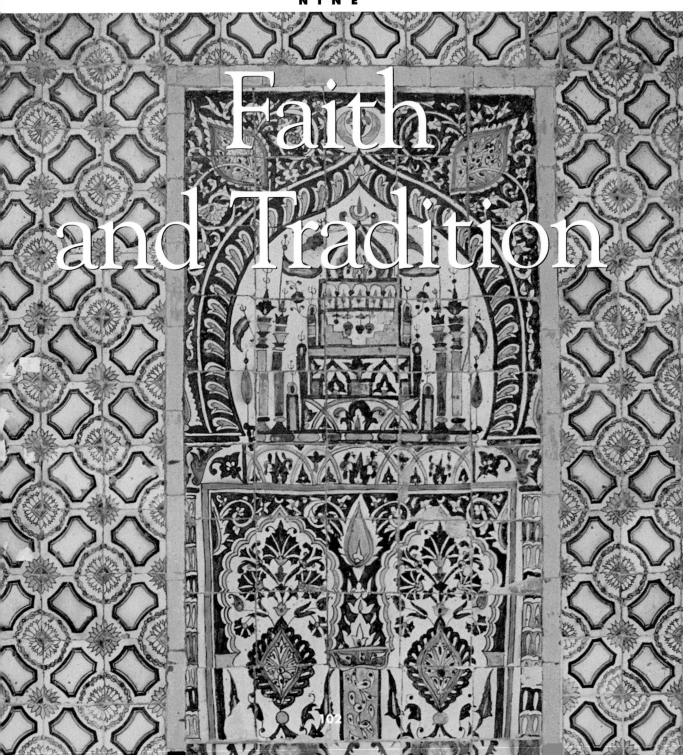

Faith and Tradition

Opposite: **Muslim art on the walls of a mosque**

L IBYAN CULTURE, LIKE MOST OF LIBYAN LIFE, IS BASED ON THE laws of Islam. It also preserves the country's long history and rich tradition.

A beautifully decorated door in Tripoli

Libyan Art

Beautiful gold vases, intricate rugs, fancy leather goods—Libyan artists create many fine pieces. But look closely—something makes their work different from most of the artwork seen in the United States or Canada.

Following Islamic tradition, most Libyan artists do not depict humans or living creatures in their work. Allah and the prophet Muhammad are never depicted in Islamic art either. Instead, most of the traditional arts—leatherwork, metal engraving, weaving, gold and silver jewelry, pottery, and embroidery—feature elaborate geometric designs. Such designs are found on many mosques and other religious and civic buildings too.

Islamic Art

Because Muslims believe that Allah, or God, is the sole creator of life, they rarely make paintings or sculptures of humans, animals, or plants. They believe it would be trespassing on Allah's role as the creator to construct an image of a life form.

Instead, Islamic art is beautifully decorated with intricate geometric patterns and designs. These designs are called *arabesque* (Arabian ornamentation). Generally, people, plants, or animals found in the works are highly stylized and abstract, far from reality.

Festivals Add Color to Life

Libyans enjoy preserving their traditions through the festivals that take place in nearly every city. The most widely celebrated national holiday is September 1—Revolution Day—the anniversary of the Libyan Revolution in which Qaddafi overthrew King Idris. On this day, Libyans listen to many speeches and enjoy colorful parades that fill streets throughout the country.

Independence Day, celebrated on December 24, honors the day when Libya first gained its freedom from foreign control in 1951. Other national holidays include June 11—*al-Jala'a*, or Evacuation Day—which marks the day in 1970 when all foreign military bases in Libya were evacuated; August 9, Army Day; October 7, Constitution Day; and November 21, Proclamation Day.

Religious Holidays

Among the many religious holidays of Islam is Muhammad's birthday, also known as Prophet's Day, or *Moulid al-Nabawi*. This is a day when Muslims study Muhammad's words and life, and pray. In the evening, they celebrate with firecrackers, music, laughter, and delicious meals. *Eid al-Adha*, the Feast of the Sacrifice, is the most important Islamic holiday.

Ramadan, the month of fasting and the ninth month on the Islamic calendar, is an important time for Muslims. During this period, Muhammad received the first of many revelations from God. These were eventually written down and became known as the Qur'an, the holy book of Islam. The only time Muslims may eat, drink, or smoke during Ramadan is after sundown. Two more holidays are associated with it. *Lailat al-Badr,* the Night of the Full Moon, falls two weeks before Ramadan begins. It is a time to prepare for Ramadan, as Muslims say special prayers and forgive one another. A very happy festival for all is the day after the month of Ramadan ends—*Eid al-Fitr.* It is a new beginning. Muslims celebrate with decorations, delicious foods and sweets, new clothes, and gifts. They also remember the poor with charity.

Marriage Traditions

Weddings in Libya are rich in tradition. In the past, most Libyan marriages were arranged, usually when the bride was in her mid-teens and the groom was in his late twenties. Parents selected partners for their children using a matchmaker or their own social contacts. People in smaller villages preferred to find mates from the same tribe—relatives, who could be as

A wedding in Tripoli

Weeklong Weddings

Weddings in Libya are not the quick affairs they are in North America, with a brief ceremony and reception. In Libya, traditional Islamic weddings last a full week, and they are quite expensive. The groom usually pays a small, symbolic amount of money or property to the bride, to provide her with some independent wealth. Each night during the week, the bride wears a traditional Islamic dress in a different color.

For the first three days, the focus is on the bride and her female relatives and friends. They gather in the bride's home to celebrate, and to paint designs on her hands, feet, and dress using a mixture of henna and water. Bridesmaids wear these henna designs, too.

On the fourth night, the bride and groom receive their gifts, and for the next two nights, there is more singing, dancing, and eating. The actual wedding ceremony takes place in the bride's home on the sixth night, and on the seventh night, the bride goes to join the groom at his home, where she will now live. Wives keep their maiden names after marriage. It is an honor for young Libyans to have children as soon as possible after they are married.

close as first cousins, were ideal. Today, these traditions are changing, and young Libyans are demanding to choose partners for themselves. This is especially true among young city dwellers.

Men are allowed by Islamic law to take up to four wives. This rule dates back several centuries, to a time when many men died on the battlefield, and there were far more women than men. The only rule for men was that they treat each wife equally. Today, it's unusual for a man to have more than one wife. Few men can afford to take care of more than one wife. Also, a recent law requires a man to get permission from his first wife before marrying a second time. In the rare cases where a man does take two wives, it is usually because the first wife is unable to bear children, or because he is wealthy enough to take care of a large family.

Music

Just as singing and dancing are an important part of the marriage traditions in Libya, music is a part of almost all religious and social ceremonies and festivities. The music has a strong Arabic and Islamic influence. Rhythm is a very important element, so someone usually plays drums or tambourine, while others clap their hands. Other instruments include flutes made of bamboo, bells, and horns.

Songs often tell the stories of great triumphs in history or of difficult struggles faced by ancestors long ago. Some traditional folk songs handed down by the nomadic tribes speak lovingly of the desert sands, and tell of journeys across the Sahara. Simple folk dances accompany some of the songs performed during marriage ceremonies and other special occasions.

Sports

Sports are popular in Libya, though not always the same sports that are popular in the Western world. Qaddafi has banned many sports he considers too violent—judo, boxing, and bullfighting, for example. Water sports such as skiing, diving, and swimming are enjoyed along the Mediterranean coast by Libyans and guests in resort hotels. The larger cities have facilities for golf, bowling, and tennis.

Perhaps the most popular sport in Libya is soccer, a favorite of boys throughout the country. They play it in school on organized teams, and they play it with friends on the streets of large cities and oasis villages, on the desert and near the coast.

Opposite: **Libyans enjoy swimming and relaxing on the beach.**

Soccer at Benghazi Stadium

Adults play on local teams, and their games are closely followed by avid fans. University teams and professional teams compete with teams from other Arab nations.

But spectator sports are not as popular in Libya as they are in many other parts of the world. Few teams have large followings, and rarely does an individual emerge as a sports hero. The government specifically discourages spectator sports, instead encouraging citizens to participate in sports themselves. In the *Green Book*, Qaddafi compares sports to prayer—an activity in which every individual should take part, and not just watch others participate. He writes: "Public sport is for the masses. It is a right of all people for their health and recreational benefit. It is mere stupidity to leave its benefits to certain individuals and teams who monopolize these while the masses provide the facilities and pay the expenses for the establishment of public sports. The thousands who crowd stadiums to view, applaud, and laugh are foolish people who have failed to carry out the activity themselves."

Libya and the Olympics

Libya has had an unusual history with the Olympics. After the country achieved independence in 1951, it was eager to improve its sporting abilities and to show them off at the Olympics. Libya sent its first group of three athletes to the 1968 Summer Games, held in Mexico City. They didn't bring home any medals. The next year, Qaddafi took over the country. He wished to rid the country of Western influence, so Libya sent no athletes to the 1972 Summer Games in Munich, Germany. It sent trouble instead.

Several Palestinian Arab terrorists sneaked into the Olympic Village where the athletes stayed. They took members of the Israeli team hostage and murdered eleven young athletes. Because the weapons the terrorists used had been smuggled into Germany inside Libyan diplomatic baggage, investigators determined that the Libyan government played some role in the attack. Three terrorists were captured, and three others escaped to Libya. Five terrorists were killed during the incident, and Qaddafi honored them, calling them "martyr heroes," for their roles in killing the Israeli athletes. They were buried with full military honors.

Libya's next Olympic presence came twenty years later, when a small group of athletes was sent to the 1992 Summer Games in Barcelona, Spain. Again, they earned no medals. Libya did not participate in the 1996 Summer Games in Atlanta, Georgia.

Horses and Racing

Horses are at the heart of many sporting events in Libya. People ride them in races or race in chariots behind the horses. Sometimes good horsemen participate in *fantasias*—exciting displays of their skills. They also enjoy racing special camels bred for this sport, the *mehari*.

Breeding and raising horses are important activities in Libya. The strong, graceful animals have been part of the culture for more than 3,000 years. After Islam swept through Libya, care of horses became even more important. Muhammad was defeated in a battle in 625 because he did not have enough horses. That defeat explains the importance still placed on horses in Libya today.

Libyan Media

Modern Standard Arabic is the form of Arabic taught in schools and used in formal speeches, government publications, and by the press. Traditional folktales and literature, however, are often written in an older style known as Classical Arabic. Classical Arabic is also the form used in the Qur'an.

Libyan Theater

Movie theaters are found in most major Libyan cities, but they are not as common as in many other parts of the world. There are no live theaters or concert halls. This is because Qaddafi takes the same dim view of these activities as he does of spectator sports. In the *Green Book,* he explains his philosophy that life is to be lived, not watched, just as sports are to be played, not watched. "Those who direct the course of life for themselves have no need to watch life working through actors on the stage or in the cinemas."

Opposite: **Libyans like to ride and race horses.**

An Influential Woman

Khadijah al-Jahmi contributed much to the culture of Libya, her homeland. She was born in Benghazi in 1921. As a young girl, she enjoyed writing folk poems to share with her father. He was pleased with her talent, and hired private tutors for her. For most Libyans at this time, educating girls was not a priority. But Khadijah showed great promise.

In 1955, when she was thirty-four, she became very popular as Libya's first radio anchorwoman. Publishing was Khadijah's next career. In 1966, she started a women's issues magazine called *al-Mar'ah,* which means *The Woman*. A few years later, she started a magazine dedicated to children, called *al-Amal (Hope)*. She also founded an organization for children under age six who have great artistic abilities.

Though she died in 1996, she is still remembered by many Libyans as a person who fought to give women and children a voice in the culture of their country.

Classical Arabic is not easily understood by young people. It is difficult for Libyans to find much good reading material, particularly for children.

The government is trying to correct this by providing reading material that is suitable for children. But it can take a long time to bring a book to print in Libya. The government must approve all written material before it can be published. If something is found to be objectionable to the government reviewers, the whole project is scrapped.

No foreign books, magazines, or newspapers may be brought into the country. Libyans are free to read only the one daily newspaper published in Libya, called *The New Dawn*, as well as twenty-one magazines and books from three publishing companies. All are government-owned.

Libyans with radios and television sets can hear and watch programming approved by the government. Most people have radios and about one-third have TV. Most programs begin with a reading from Qaddafi's *Green Book*. On one TV channel, all the programs are about the *Green Book*. Other channels show imported programs that have been carefully edited by government reviewers.

Libya has several museums, mostly located in the western region of the country, and all under government control. The Archaeological Museum, the Natural History Museum, the Leptis Magna Museum of Antiquities, the Sabha Museum, and the Sabratha Museum of Antiquities all contain important collections showcasing the rich history, art, and culture of Libya.

Libya's
Changing
Society

Opposite: **The city of Tripoli at sunset**

LIBYA IS IN A TIME OF CHANGE. THE COUNTRY IS MOVING between traditional and modern ways, between rural and urban lifestyles, and between poor and wealthy times.

Women in Libyan Society

The role of Libyan women has shifted much in recent decades. Traditionally, women were second-class citizens who could not vote and frequently were treated as their husbands' property.

Women attend the University of Benghazi.

But since the early 1960s, Libyan women have had the right to vote and participate in politics. When Qaddafi came into power in 1969, he further promoted equality among all citizens, and women received even greater rights. They can now serve in the military and attend universities. Traditional Muslim beliefs, however, still work to keep women in an inferior position in Libyan society.

A Libyan woman in traditional clothes

Traditional lifestyles dictate that women wear veils in public to cover their faces, allowing them to see with only one eye. Women who keep these traditions have their own part of the home where no men—except close male relatives—can ever go. If they are wealthy, they rarely leave their homes unescorted by relatives. When they do, they walk in pairs and avoid contact with men. This way of life is more common in urban areas. In rural areas, the demands of farming require women to live and work more equally alongside men.

But even among urban women, especially younger Libyans, the traditional lifestyle is mainly a thing of the past. Few women under forty wear the veil. Instead, they wear colorful dresses, or skirts with blouses. Women get out in public, attending school and holding jobs. Still, they are steered strongly toward "women's work," such as teaching and social work. And they are still expected to have children and raise them at home without outside help. Many women are caught in the middle of this shift in the role of women—following some old ways out of a sense of duty, while trying to live a more modern life.

Men's Lives Change, Too

Libyan society has always granted men more authority and rights than women, and this too is changing, but slowly. Men still hold most jobs outside the home, but now they work in factories and offices, in construction, and on the oil fields. Few work as farmers today.

Clothing has changed for men too. No longer do most younger urban men wear the long, flowing white robes that for centuries were associated with Islam. Nor do most wear turbans—long scarves wrapped around their heads. Instead, many men have adopted Western fashions, even T-shirts and jeans, or suits for business. Others wear long, loose tunics and slacks with sandals. In the desert however, the long flowing robes are still the norm. Nothing works better for staying cool and keeping the sand out.

The men's floor in a department store in Tripoli

National Holidays in Libya

Declaration of the Jamahiriya (the People's Authority)	March 2
Evacuation of Foreign Military Bases	June 11
Army Day	August 9
Revolution Day	September 1
Constitution Day	October 7
Day of Mourning	October 26
Proclamation Day	November 21
Independence Day	December 24

A Home for Every Family

Today, most young couples strike out on their own if they can afford it. They no longer live with the groom's parents, as was once the custom. But traditional homes still contain many extended family members. An extended family may include a husband and wife, their unmarried children, married sons with their families, and other unmarried female family members, such as mothers and sisters.

The move from rural life to city life has happened rapidly, and in some places, cities have not kept up with their growing populations. As a result, some large, extended families must live together. Housing is cramped, the streets and public areas are dirty, and fresh food—fruits and vegetables, meat, milk, and eggs—are often hard to come by.

Life in the City

Nevertheless, the city usually offers at least the chance of a better life. Although education is compulsory for all Libyan children, schools are more available in cities than in remote rural areas. All children must attend elementary school from age six to age twelve. In elementary schools, boys and girls study together, but as they get older, boys and girls are separated.

After elementary school, students attend intermediate school, where studies center on Arabic, the Qur'an, Islam, history, geography, and science. After age 15, education is no

longer compulsory. Then the students have the option of enrolling in three years of high school, followed by college, in either Tripoli, Benghazi, or Sabha. Or they may choose to

Children recite verses of the Qur'an at the Al Eman Nafeh Qur'anic School in Tripoli.

No Freedom of Speech

The freedom of speech we enjoy in the United States and Canada—the ability to criticize and question our governments and leaders and to speak our own minds without fearing punishment—is something citizens don't have in Libya. They especially dare not criticize Qaddafi, for he has been known to imprison people who spoke out against the Libyan government.

attend vocational school instead, for training in agriculture, technology, and other careers.

Because of the mandatory schooling, the literacy rate in Libya has improved greatly. In 1951, illiteracy was about 90 percent, and girls were not allowed an education beyond elementary school. But along with the discovery of oil came enough money to fund better schools in Libya, free to all children. Today, less than 25 percent of the population is illiterate, and that number continues to drop.

National Unity

Despite the many social changes of recent decades, and the varied lifestyles led by Libyans today, some things bind them all together as a nation. Perhaps the most common thread running through the lives of most Libyans is their devotion to Islam. Family is important to all Libyans too. They enjoy their time together—talking, playing games, and sharing meals.

A Flair for Flavor

Libyans seem to love spicy foods, particularly breads and pastas with fiery seasonings, but the accompaniments usually vary, depending on the location in Libya. People near the

لا إستقلال لِشِعب
يأكُ... وراى البَحر

Game Time

Among the games Libyans enjoy are chess and domi-noes. In a Bedouin game popular in the desert, a grid is drawn in the sand. Players take turns placing a marker in a square, and try to get three in a row. When they do, they can take an opponent's marker. *Isseren* is an easy game, popular with children. Players take turns throwing six sticks, each split lengthwise, into the air, then count how many land with the split side up.

Vegetable couscous with tomato cilantro sauce

coast eat some seafood, but fish is not generally eaten in Libya. Bedouins eat more camel meat.

Libyan food has several influences—Arabic, of course, and Mediterranean, due to their geography, but there is also some Italian. This dates back to the early 1900s, when Italians controlled Libya. Most Libyans hated the Italians because of their cruelty during this period, but they liked their food. Pasta is particularly popular.

Dining Style

Libyans pray before and after each meal. They often eat with the fingers of their right hand instead of with silverware. Guests eat first at a meal, followed by the oldest family members. Little talking is done during meals. Traditionally, men and women ate separately, but this is less common today in urban areas. Most families simply don't have enough room in their homes for two dining spaces.

Opposite: **Hummus, pita, and dried fruit**

Few Libyans eat at restaurants—these are usually visited by foreigners. Libyans prefer to eat at home, or enjoy picnics at the seaside on Fridays, their weekly holiday.

A Libyan staple at many meals, *couscous*, is a form of pasta, but it seems more like rice than noodles. The dough is rolled until it forms small, round crumbs. These are steamed like rice, and usually topped with a meat-and-vegetable mixture. Lamb is the most popular meat, but sometimes chicken or beef

Libyans celebrate prospects of the future in the Great Man-Made River.

is eaten with couscous. Pork is never eaten, as the Qur'an does not allow it.

Olives, apricots, oranges, and figs—and dishes that feature them—often round out meals. Salt and various peppers are the most common spices in Libyan dishes, but ginger and cinnamon are also used, as are garlic and cumin.

Libyans enjoy soft drinks and bottled mineral water, and fruit juices are popular in season. But tea and coffee are probably the most common beverages in the country. Green tea is served hot— some say Libyans drink more tea per person than any other people. Coffee is served very thick and sweet.

While the Libyan diet is generally flavorful, it suffers from a lack of variety because few fruits or vegetables can be grown on the dry land. But if Qaddafi's Great Man-Made River works out and Libyans tap into the water flowing underground, it will certainly mean a greater variety of foods on their tables, and another great change in Libyan lifestyles.

Timeline

Libyan History

People are living in what is now Libya.	**c. 8000** B.C.
Berbers are living in what is now Libya.	**c. 3000** B.C.
Phoenicians establish ports in Tripolitania.	**1300** B.C.
Rome gains control of Tripolitania.	**46** B.C.
The Vandals conquer what is now Libya.	**435** A.D.
The Arabs take control and bring Islam to what is now Libya.	**643**
Spain gains control of Libya.	**1510**
Ottoman Turks take control of Libya.	**1551 — 1911**

World History

c. 2500 B.C.	Egyptians build the Pyramids and Sphinx in Giza.
563 B.C.	Buddha is born in India.
A.D. **313**	The Roman emperor Constantine recognizes Christianity.
610	The prophet Muhammad begins preaching a new religion called Islam.
1054	The Eastern (Orthodox) and Western (Roman) Churches break apart.
1066	William the Conqueror defeats the English in the Battle of Hastings.
1095	Pope Urban II proclaims the First Crusade.
1215	King John seals the Magna Carta.
1300s	The Renaissance begins in Italy.
1347	The Black Death sweeps through Europe.
1453	Ottoman Turks capture Constantinople, conquering the Byzantine Empire.
1492	Columbus arrives in North America.
1500s	The Reformation leads to the birth of Protestantism.

Libyan History

U.S. Navy defeats the Barbary pirates at Tripoli.	**1805**
Sidi Muhammad ibn-Ali establishes the Sanusi brotherhood, strengthening beliefs of Muslims in Libya.	**1837**
Libya comes under Italy's control.	**1911**
The Libyan Arab Force helps the British fight the Italians and Germans in Libya during World War II.	**1939 —** **1945**
Libya becomes an independant nation, the United Kingdom of Libya, under the rule of King Idris.	**1951**
Vast oil fields are discovered in Libya.	**1959**
Libyan army officers overthrow King Idris; Libya becomes the Libyan Arab Republic under the control of Muammar al-Qaddafi.	**1969**
Libya is renamed the Socialist People's Libyan Arab Jamahiriya.	**1977**
The Libyan air force attacks U.S. military planes over the Mediterranean; two Libyan planes are downed.	**1981**
The United States imposes trade sanctions on Libya.	**1982**
Work begins on the Great Man-Made River.	**1984**
The United States bombs parts of Tripoli and Benghazi.	**1986**
Pan Am Flight 103 blows up over Lockerbie, Scotland; Libyan terrorists are believed to have planted a bomb on the plane.	**1988**
Two Libyans are charged in a U.S. court with planting the bomb; Qaddafi refuses to turn over the Libyans for trial.	**1991**
The United Nations bans air travel to and from Libya.	**1992**
Two Libyan suspects in Flight 103 bombing are turned over for trial in the Netherlands; UN sanctions are suspended.	**1999**

World History

1776	The Declaration of Independence is signed.
1789	The French Revolution begins.
1865	The American Civil War ends.
1914	World War I breaks out.
1917	The Bolshevik Revolution brings Communism to Russia.
1929	Worldwide economic depression begins.
1939	World War II begins, following the German invasion of Poland.
1957	The Vietnam War starts.
1989	The Berlin Wall is torn down, as Communism crumbles in Eastern Europe.
1996	Bill Clinton reelected U.S. president.

Fast Facts

Socialist People's Libyan Arab Jamahiriya

Capital: Tripoli

Official language: Arabic

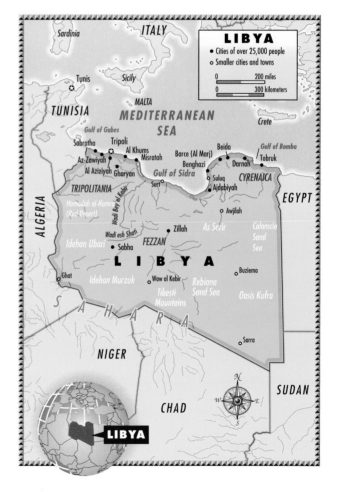

Libyan flag

Official religion:	Islam
Founding date:	1951, United Kingdom of Libya; 1969, Libyan Arab Republic
Founder:	Muammar al-Qaddafi
National anthem:	*Allahu Akbar Fawqa Kayd Al-Motadi* ("God Is Greater Than the Aggressor's Malice")
Government:	Socialist state with one policy-making body, the General People's Congress
Chief of state:	No formal office exists.
Head of government:	Secretary of the General People's Committee
Area and Dimensions:	679,358 square miles (1,759,401 sq km); 930 miles (1,497 km) north to south; 1,050 miles (1,690 km) east to west
Coordinates of geographic center:	25° North, 17° East
Land and water borders:	Mediterranean Sea to the north; Egypt to the east; Sudan to the southeast; Chad and Niger to the south; Algeria and Tunisia to the west
Highest elevation:	Bikku Bitti (Bette Peak), 7,500 feet (2,286 m) above sea level
Lowest elevation:	Sabkhat Ghuzayyil, 154 feet (47 m) below sea level
Average temperature extremes:	88°F (31°C), at Sabha, in July; 47°F (8°C), at Tripoli, in January
Average precipitation extremes:	16 inches (40 cm), near Tripoli; less than 1 inch (2.5 cm), in the Sahara

Oasis

National population (1998 est.):	5,690,727
Population (1998 est.) of four largest cities:	Tripoli 591,100 Benghazi 446,250 Misratah 121,700 Az-Zawiyah 89,338

Famous landmarks: *Cyrene* (east of Benghazi)
Ghadames (near the borders with Algeria and Tunisia)
Leptis Magna (near Tripoli)
The Marble Arch (Tripoli)
Sabratha (near Tripoli)
Tadrart Acacus (near Ghat)
Tripoli Castle/The Red Castle (Tripoli)

Industry: Libya's economy is based on the petroleum industry. Most of the country's earnings from foreign trade come from oil sales. Petroleum products and chemicals made from petroleum are Libya's most important manufactured goods. Other leading manufactured goods are cement, steel, and processed foods. Although the government controls most industries, individuals have been encouraged to start their own businesses in recent years.

Currency: The Libyan dinar is Libya's basic monetary unit. 1999 exchange rate: 1 dinar = U.S.$2.22 (U.S.$1 = 0.45 dinar)

5 dinars

Weights and measures: Libya officially uses the metric system. However, other weights and measures are also used, such as the *oke* (3 pounds, or 1.36 kg) and the *draa* (18 inches, or 46 cm).

Literacy:	76% (1995)	

Common Arabic words and phrases:		
	aiwa or *naam*	yes
	akl	food
	assalamu alákum	hello
	bikam	How much?
	bisalama	good-bye
	ismah-lee	excuse me
	kam kilometri	How far to . . . ?
	keef halek	How are you?
	khubz	bread
	la	no
	mesjeed	mosque
	min fadlek	please
	moyyah	water
	qahwa	coffee
	shukran	Thank-you.
	wain	where

Famous People:

Khadijah al-Jahmi (1921–1996)
Activist for women and children

Omar al-Mukhtar (1862–1931)
Resistance leader

Muammar al-Qaddafi (1942–   )
Political leader

Sidi Muhammad ibn Ali al-Sanusi (1787–1859)
Religious leader

Mohammed Idris al-Senussi (1890–1983)
First king

Muammar al-Qaddafi

To Find Out More

Nonfiction

▶ Forester, C. S. *The Barbary Pirates*. New York: Random House, 1953.

▶ Gottfried, Ted. *Libya: Desert Land in Conflict*. Brookfield, Conn.: Millbook Press, 1994.

Biography

▶ Kyle, Benjamin. *Muammar el-Qaddafi*. New York: Chelsea House Publishers, 1989.

▶ Malcolm, Peter. *Libya*. New York: Marshall Cavendish, 1993.

▶ Spencer, William. *Global Studies: The Middle East*. Guilford, Conn.: Dushkin Publishing Group, 1988.

Websites

▶ **arab.net**

http://www.arab.net/libya/libya_
contents.html

*Offers a variety of information on
Libya and other Arab countries in the
Middle East and North Africa.*

▶ **Libyana**

http://www.libyana.org/

*A cultural site with impressive graphics
maintained by Libyan men and
women. Departments include art,
crafts, poetry, music, people, history,
and interactive functions such as
forums, chats, and related links.*

▶ **Libya—A Country Study**

http://lcweb2.loc.gov/frd/cs/lytoc.html

*A detailed study from the Library of
Congress on a variety of Libyan topics*

Organizations and Embassies

▶ **General Board of Tourism**
P.O. Box 71981
Tripoli, Libya

▶ **Permanent Mission of the Socialist
People's Libyan Arab Jamahiriya to
the United Nations**
http://www.undp.org/missions/libya

▶ **Middle East Outreach Council
(MEOC)**
University of Pennsylvania
838 Williams Hall
Philadelphia, PA 19143-6305
(215) 898-4690 or (215) 898-6335

Index

Page numbers in *italics* indicate illustrations.

literacy rate, 122
literature, 31, 113–114
livestock, 78, *78*. *See also* agriculture.

M
Mandela, Nelson, 66, *66*
manufacturing, 70–71, *70*, 77, 79, *79*
maps. *See also* historical maps.
    Carthage, *41*
    ethnic groups, *84*
    geopolitical, *9*
    Italian acquisitions, *51*
    natural resources, *24*
    population distribution, 89
    Roman Empire, *43*
    spread of Islam, *48*
    topographical, *18*
    Tripoli, *60*
    Vandal Empire, *45*
marabouts, 96
marine life, 78, 124
marriage, 106–107, *106*
Mawlay Mohamed Mosque, 95
Mecca, 91, 93, *93*, 99, *99*
Mediterranean Sea, 13, *16*, 17, 19, 27
Megrahi, Abdel Basset Ali, 64
military, 13, 62, *62*, 64, 80, 118
mining, 77
Misratah, 24, 88
mosques (Islamic house of worship), 98, *101*, *102*, *104*
movie theaters, 113
Muhammad (Islamic prophet), 91
Mujahedeen (Freedom Fighters), 51
al-Mukhtar, Omar, 51, 133
museums, 115
music, 108

N
national coat of arms, 71
national flag, 61, *61*, *101*
national holidays, 120
    Independence Day, 104–105
    Revolution Day, 104
natural resources map, *24*
The New Dawn (newspaper), 114
New Socialism. *See* Third Universal
    Theory.
Night of the Full Moon. *See Lailat al-Badr*.
nomads, 22, 25, 31, 84, 85, 86, *86*, 108
Norman Crusaders, 48

O
oases, 8, 22, *22*, 36, 76, 77, 86
oil industry, 8, 11–12, *12*, 64, 67, 69, 74–75, *74*, 83
Old City, 83
Olympic Games, 111

P
Pan American Flight 103, 63–64. *See also* terrorism.
people, 26, 67, 80, 82, *109*, 123, *126–127*. *See also* Famous people.
    Almohads, 48
    Arabs, 45, 81
    Bedouin nomads, 22, 86–87
    Berbers, 40, 86–87
    Carthaginians, 41–42, 92
    children, *17*, 22, 81, *121*
    clothing, 86, 87, *118*
    dehydration, 26
    dining style, 124
    education, 70, 89, 120, 122
    employment, 70–72
    ethnic groups map, *84*
    funerals, 97
    Garamantes, 40
    Greeks, 42–43
    health care, 64, 70, 89
    housing, 13, 47, 77, 88, 120
    infant mortality rate, 82
    literacy rate, 122
    marabouts, 96
    marriage, 106–107, *106*
    men, 58, 99, 119
    Muslims, 45
    nomads, 22, 25, 31, 84, 85, 86, *86*, 108
    Norman Crusaders, 48
    Phoenicians, 40–41
    Romans, 42–43
    sharifs, 96
    Shiite Muslims, 94

Meet the Author

TERRI WILLIS LEARNED TO LOVE BOOKS WHEN SHE WAS READ to every day by her mother while growing up in Minnesota. "I've always loved to escape into books," she says. "Sometimes, when I was a kid, I'd be reading three or four of them at a time, and I always brought books and a flashlight under the covers with me at night." Now, it's a thrill for her to be able to write books for a new generation of readers.

She begins researching her topic in her local library, checking out the information available there. Usually there's a lot in the reference collections and on the stacks. Encyclopedias are good starting points, too, she says, giving her a brief understanding of the topic.

From there, it becomes a matter of filling in the blanks—adding the detail that can make a book exciting and loaded with neat information. She hunts down materials from government agencies and other organizations, hits the Internet

for up-to-minute facts, and sorts through the collections of major libraries on university campuses and in large cities. "I love searching out the details," Terri says. "I especially like hanging out in big libraries. To me, it's like panning for gold. There's usually a lot to sort through, but occasionally you find that great nugget of a fact that really adds to the book."

Terri got her degree in journalism at the University of Wisconsin—Madison. She is the author of eight books for children and young adults, mostly on geography and the environment, including two for the Children's Press series Saving Planet Earth—*Land Use and Abuse* and *Cars: An Environmental Challenge*, which she co-wrote with Wallace B. Black. She's also written for a geography newsletter and several newspapers and magazines. She lives in Cedarburg, Wisconsin, with her husband, Harry, and their two young daughters, Andrea and Elizabeth, who are read to every day!

Photo Credits